LARGE PRINT
PRINT
Devotions

Print ISBN 978-1-63609-847-0

Text is compiled from the Daily Wisdom for Women series, published by Barbour Publishing.

Published by Barbour Publishing, Inc., 1810 Barbour Drive, Uhrichsville, Ohio 44683, www.barbourbooks.com

Our mission is to inspire the world with the life-changing message of the Bible.

Printed in China.

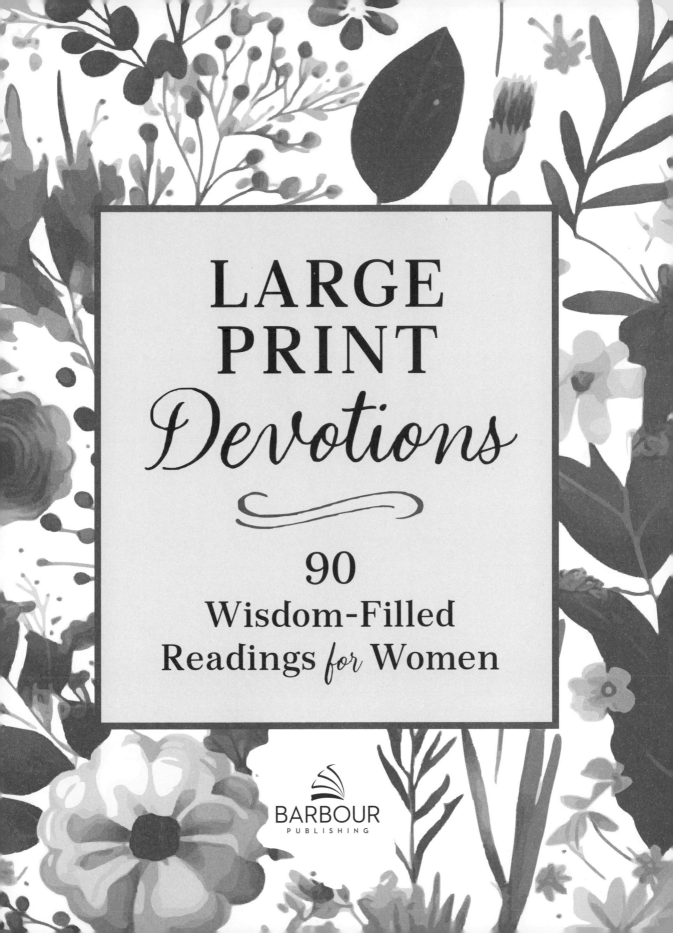

LARGE PRINT
Devotions

90
Wisdom-Filled
Readings *for* Women

BARBOUR
PUBLISHING

INTRODUCTION

Joyful is the person who finds wisdom, the one who gains understanding. For wisdom is more profitable than silver, and her wages are better than gold. Wisdom is more precious than rubies; nothing you desire can compare with her. She offers you long life in her right hand, and riches and honor in her left. She will guide you down delightful paths; all her ways are satisfying. Wisdom is a tree of life to those who embrace her; happy are those who hold her tightly.

PROVERBS 3:13–18 NLT

Experience an intimate connection to your heavenly Father in these wisdom-filled readings for your heart.

Each spread features a powerful devotional reading and prayer, perfect for everyday inspiration and encouragement. Enhance your spiritual journey with these refreshing readings, grow in wisdom, deepen your faith—and come to know just how deeply and tenderly God loves you.

THE SMALL, RIGHT, KIND THING

[Joseph of Arimathea] went to Pilate and asked for the body of Jesus. Then he took it down and wrapped it in a linen shroud and laid him in a tomb cut in stone, where no one had ever yet been laid.

LUKE 23:52–53 ESV

Joseph of Arimathea never felt right about how the other members of the Jewish high council plotted against Jesus. Later, when the council handed Jesus over to Pilate, Joseph knew it meant a death sentence for the seemingly rebellious Rabbi. Although Joseph felt certain it was wrong, he was also powerless to stop it. And what good would it do if *he* ended up on a cross next to Jesus?

This world is full of injustice—from bullying on the playground to sexism to favoritism to racism. Often we

can and should take a stand against it, but there are times that we can't. But that doesn't mean we shouldn't do *anything*.

Take a lesson from Joseph of Arimathea. He couldn't do the big thing (saving Jesus' life), but he *could* do the small, right, kind thing by giving Jesus' body a proper burial and place to rest. God used Joseph as part of His perfect plan of salvation. And in that light, it was no small thing!

God, when I am not able to do the big thing, give me eyes to see the small, right, kind thing. And use that small thing to result in big things for You! Amen.

OPEN MOUTH

Everyone enjoys a fitting reply; it is wonderful to say the right thing at the right time!
PROVERBS 15:23 NLT

Open mouth, insert foot.

We've all known the taste of toe jam. We're too quick to speak and woefully shortsighted when we're being insensitive. James 3:2 tells us that if we could control our tongues, we would be perfect and could also control ourselves in every other way. But we aren't perfect, and our words indicate just that.

So how can you become a woman known for saying the right thing at the right time?

1. Hold your tongue. "Too much talk leads to sin. Be sensible and keep your mouth shut" (Proverbs 10:19 NLT).

2. Ask God for words. "Take control of what I say, O LORD, and guard my lips" (Psalm 141:3 NLT).

3. In all words, love. "Most important of all, continue to show deep love for each other, for love covers a multitude of sins" (1 Peter 4:8 NLT).

God's grace covers your sins, including the words that come out of your mouth. Getting a handle on your tongue—making your responses fitting and kind and good and helpful—is a spiritual discipline that won't happen overnight. But with work and with God's help, you can be transformed into a woman known for saying the right thing at the right time!

God, help me tame this wild, unpredictable thing inside my mouth. I can't do it alone. Amen.

SIMPLE LIVING

A wise person is hungry for knowledge,
while the fool feeds on trash.
PROVERBS 15:14 NLT

In today's world, there's no lack of diversion to fill our eyes, ears, heads, and hearts. Books and magazines are only the beginning. From traditional TV and movies to streaming music and videos, video games, podcasts, audiobooks, blogs, social media, and every other rabbit hole, we can access lifetimes of information through the touch screen grasped tightly in our fists.

If we're honest, much of what we take in has no lasting value. And what seems harmless, simply trivial and fluffy, can do real damage to our spiritual health and heart. Most of it is *garbage*. Proverbs calls one who feasts on this trash a *fool*.

The wise person, instead, is hungry for knowledge—for ideas and entertainment that promote good in the

world and will encourage one to pursue good as well. Where can you go to fill your hunger? The first and best answer is to God's Word, but there are so many other resources that are rooted in good and available to you as well. When you find one, recommend it to others— spread knowledge and take out the trash!

Father, I'm grateful for knowledge at my fingertips. Give me a hunger for the good and a distaste for trash. Amen.

REAL LOVE

*Carry each other's burdens, and in this
way you will fulfill the law of Christ.*
GALATIANS 6:2 NIV

Jesus summed up all of God's law in two simple commandments: love God; love others (Matthew 22:36–40).

But what does it really mean to *love others*? How do we take this seemingly simple command and do it?

Jesus explained practical, day-to-day love this way: love your neighbor as you love yourself (Mark 12:31). If that idea seems too abstract (because some days we're not sure we *like* ourselves, let alone *love* ourselves), Jesus says to treat others the way you would like to be treated (Luke 6:31).

Paul makes loving others even more practical in Galatians 6:2 when he tells us that we love others when we carry their burdens. That means *noticing* when someone in our sphere is having a hard time.

Who in your life is stumbling under some circumstance or stress? Even if you can't solve the problem, what action can you take to ease their struggle, to help them stand firm? Maybe it's running errands, making a week's worth of freezer meals, taking a friend out for coffee and offering a listening ear. Carrying another's burden is tangible evidence of your love for others and love of God's ways.

Father, because of Your great love for me, I want to love others the same way. Show me opportunities to carry the burdens of others. Make me strong in You to help in big ways and small. Amen.

WHAT GOD THINKS OF IDOLS

The whole human race is foolish and has no knowledge! The craftsmen are disgraced by the idols they make, for their carefully shaped works are a fraud. These idols have no breath or power. Idols are worthless; they are ridiculous lies! On the day of reckoning they will all be destroyed.

JEREMIAH 51:17–18 NLT

Twenty-first-century idols look different than the idols of Old Testament times. Where pagan craftsmen once made figures for worship out of precious metals, wood, and stone, our idols are made out of much more sophisticated materials. Consider:

- The sleek steel body and rich leather interior of a brand-new vehicle

- The precision-cut glass, cobalt, graphite, lithium, silicon, and aluminum of a smartphone

- The wood, drywall, stone, marble, metal, and glass of a magazine-ready house

- The oxygen, carbon, hydrogen, nitrogen, calcium, and phosphorus that make up the human body (idols included but not limited to: our children, husbands, a celebrity, or even our own bodies)

Is there anything or anyone more important in your life than God? Do those worthless idols hold more influence than God in your life because you spend more time on them than on your relationship with Him? Remember, living a real life and obtaining real wisdom comes from worshipping God the transformer, not the transformed.

God, You are better than anything I could ever put in Your place! Forgive my wayward heart. I want You and You only. Amen.

CONFIDENT HOPE

*I pray that your hearts will be flooded with light
so that you can understand the confident hope
he has given to those he called—his holy people
who are his rich and glorious inheritance.*

Ephesians 1:18 nlt

"I hope it doesn't rain."

"I hope the meeting today is short."

"I hope I can find a dress for the wedding this weekend."

We often use the word *hope* as a vague, "Gee, I'd like something to turn out in my favor" wish. But the confident hope Paul is praying for the believers in Ephesians 1:18–19 is a powerful, life-giving gift from God that's available to us today.

Faith-filled hope allows an individual to thrive in the face of a grim diagnosis. Reliance on the goodness of God's plan helps families endure financial hardships.

The light of Christ keeps parents of prodigal children from despair. God's holy people know, even when the entire world is in turmoil, they have confident and unshakable hope in the Father.

Have you grasped hold of God's gift of hope? Just as Paul prayed for the Ephesians, ask God to flood your heart with light and give you greater understanding of this priceless gift. Our confidence grows when we remind ourselves of the ways He provided in the past and how He sustains us in the present—leading us to a future fully relying on Him, come what may.

*Gift-Giving God, every day I
choose Your confident hope.*

GOD CONFIDENCE

When God our Savior revealed his kindness and love, he saved us, not because of the righteous things we had done, but because of his mercy. He washed away our sins, giving us a new birth and new life through the Holy Spirit. . . . Because of his grace he made us right in his sight and gave us confidence that we will inherit eternal life.

TITUS 3:4–5, 7 NLT

When do you feel most confident? Whether it's some aspect of your career or ministry or hobby, your confidence shines brightest when you're doing something you're exceptionally good at. Confidence is empowering. Confidence is a great feeling.

But none of us is perfect, and we all have bad days that cause us to question if we know what we're doing. Setbacks can leave us frustrated and wondering why we even try.

That's why God's grace is so important in every aspect in our lives. Our old lives had moments of greatness, but ultimately were empty and worthless. Our new lives when we're born again are perfect and whole because Jesus Christ is perfect and whole. So we never have to wonder if we're good enough or if our self-confidence can carry us through. Our God confidence empowers us in this moment and through all of eternity.

*Father, fill me with the God confidence that
I need today. Let Your mercy and grace fill
my heart and my soul. Breathe in me a new
life every moment of every day. Amen.*

HOLY HEALTH

A peaceful heart leads to a healthy body;
jealousy is like cancer in the bones.
PROVERBS 14:30 NLT

What are your current health goals? Maybe you're trying to be more active or eat healthier to shed a few pounds. Perhaps eight-hours-per-night sleep is your aim. De-stress or detox? HIIT or Fitbit? Delivery or DiGiorno?

It's easy to get discouraged by the ever-changing requirements of a "healthy lifestyle." For, as Christians, we know someday God will give us new bodies (1 Corinthians 15:35–58; 2 Corinthians 5:1–5), so appointments with the treadmill may feel like an exercise in futility (pun intended). But God cares about your physical state—values your body so much that His Holy Spirit has *chosen* to take up residence there. Paul goes on to say in 1 Corinthians 6:19–20, "You do not belong

to yourself, for God bought you with a high price. So you must honor God with your body" (NLT).

Honoring God with your body starts with obeying His Word. Many of the spiritual disciplines Jesus teaches are soul matters. But a healthy spirit and soul, confidently standing in God's grace can cultivate a contented heart, stronger relationships with friends and family, restful sleep, less stress, and a more positive outlook—all of which can have an impact on your physical health, both now and in the long term.

Father, give me the motivation I need to treat my earthly body as a precious gift from You. Amen.

EXPERT CRAFTSMANSHIP

Together, we are his house, built on the foundation of the apostles and the prophets. And the cornerstone is Christ Jesus himself. We are carefully joined together in him, becoming a holy temple for the Lord.

EPHESIANS 2:20–21 NLT

YouTube is full of step-by-step how-to videos for any home project. From framing a wall to installing a toilet O-ring, any novice with an internet connection can arm herself with information to tackle a project. But simply knowing the steps doesn't make the novice an expert, and without experience and guidance from a seasoned pro, a simple Saturday project can derail quickly.

Have you ever felt this way in your own faith? Are you hoping for growth and change but seeing little? Heart and soul renovation, like home renovation, works

better alongside seasoned experts.

As the church, we are apprentices in the perfectly crafted house of God. As a work-in-progress for more than 2,000 years, Jesus Himself is not only the foundational cornerstone, He's the foreman, chief architect, and on-the-job trainer who teaches us how to build relationships, love others, and do His good work on earth. We're joined together as His crew as we continue to build and strengthen His house on the generations of believers who came before us.

Jesus, when I feel isolated in my faith,
remind me that I'm an important apprentice
in the building of Your church. Bring mentors
into my life who'll help me grow in my faith
and maintain an unshakable trust in You.

LEARN FROM THE BEST

My son, obey your father's commands, and don't neglect your mother's instruction. Keep their words always in your heart.
PROVERBS 6:20–21 NLT

Remember when your mom knew nothing? When she couldn't *possibly* understand what you were going through or what you were feeling?

And then, one day, she did.

Today maybe you're in the Mom-who-knows-nothing role, doing your best to lovingly guide your child through the growing-up years. Even though life experience has gained you the wisdom to offer real help, that help can fall on deaf ears. (But don't give up, Mama! Keep on loving those deaf ears!)

Proverbs 6:20–21 may be directed toward a youthful

reader, but each of us can learn from the wisdom in these verses. No matter our age, we can seek out godly mentors. They may be older than we are or just be further along in their faith walk, but we can learn from their experience. Do you know someone who has come through the other side of a struggle or challenge similar to your own? Ask her what she learned. Ask her what she wished she knew that she knows now and what she would change if she could do it again.

You may gain a perspective and understanding you never expected by really listening and keeping their words in your heart.

Father, show me the mentors You've placed in my life who'll speak Your truth and wisdom into my heart. I'm listening and ready to receive. Amen.

PUT YOUR MONEY WHERE YOUR FAITH IS

And I am praying that you will put into
action the generosity that comes from your
faith as you understand and experience
all the good things we have in Christ.
PHILEMON 6 NLT

Generous living starts with experiencing all the good and joyful things we have in Christ. And an outcrop of our generous *living* of this good and joyful life is our generous *giving*.

Giving. Hmm. Money is a tricky conversation for the church. Maybe we just feel like finances are too personal a topic to broach, but Jesus tells us in Matthew 6:21 that where we put our money shows where our hearts are.

Do you know where your money goes? That may

seem like a silly question, but if you can't tell where your income is going, then you aren't managing well what God has given you.

If you do know where your money goes, do the debits in your bank account line up with who you claim to be? Are you joyfully, generously giving to the church? To worthwhile organizations that do good in the world?

Let your faith overflow into your giving, and get ready to experience a more fulfilling *living* in Christ.

Father God, show me where You want me
to put Your money to use for Your kingdom.
I want to contribute in a real way! Amen.

GRANDMA'S CHINA

In a wealthy home some utensils are made of gold and silver, and some are made of wood and clay. The expensive utensils are used for special occasions, and the cheap ones are for everyday use. If you keep yourself pure, you will be a special utensil for honorable use. Your life will be clean, and you will be ready for the Master to use you for every good work.

2 TIMOTHY 2:20–21 NLT

There's something thrilling about a special occasion meal, complete with fancy dinnerware, linen napkins, and the confusing extra forks. Maybe you even associate holidays or other celebration meals with heirloom china.

In Paul's second letter to Timothy, he urges his young protégé to live a pure life so God can use him like highly prized, special occasion dinnerware—set apart for important work.

How do we live a pure life? Paul explains in 2 Timothy 2:22–24: "Flee the evil desires of youth and pursue righteousness, faith, love and peace. . . . And the Lord's servant must not be quarrelsome but must be kind to everyone, able to teach, not resentful" (NIV).

You are meant to gleam like polished silver that the master of the house is pleased to present to guests. So don't settle for being a common, everyday setting. Ask God to purify your heart and shine!

Like a priceless heirloom,
I want my life to be a special,
prized possession to You, Father. Amen.

PROPER ANGER

"In your anger do not sin": Do not let the
sun go down while you are still angry,
and do not give the devil a foothold.
Ephesians 4:26–27 niv

There's a reason we often describe anger as *fiery, white-hot, raging,* or *smoldering.* Anger can be one of the most intensely felt emotions and left unchecked can do as much damage as any wildfire. But if you read Ephesians 4:26–27 carefully, the Bible doesn't tell us that anger itself is sinful. It's what we may do *while* we're angry that may be wrong. If we react without thought, anger can injure others and wreck relationships. Anger corked up inside can cause bitterness and destroy us from the inside out.

So, what is the proper way to handle anger? Paul tells us to deal with our anger immediately—before the sun goes down—in a way that builds relationships.

Dealing with angry feelings means that we're not letting ourselves stew over them. When we work through the problem, we're not letting Satan the opportunity to divide us and let grudges take root.

Are you angry with someone today? Pray, asking God to give you the steps to take to resolve those feelings. Don't wait for another day to pass by.

God, when I am angry, help me to not react in knee-jerk ways or nurse the feeling, causing it to grow. Show me how to move through and move on.

LOVE LIKE THAT

Observe how Christ loved us. His love was not cautious but extravagant. He didn't love in order to get something from us but to give everything of himself to us. Love like that.
EPHESIANS 5:2 MSG

Jesus loves you extravagantly. Excessively. Lavishly and without limits. Abundantly, fully, and completely. The Father's love for you goes beyond affection or infatuation. It is a deep, passionate, all-consuming love—for the authentic you (Romans 5:8). There's nothing you can do to earn His love. He *is* love (1 John 4:8).

Cautious "love" sets stipulations and limits and expectations. Jesus' reckless love knows no boundaries—even to death. How can you know what love is? Jesus Christ willingly gave up His life to save yours (1 John 3:16).

He cares about your day-to-day life. He will carry

your stresses, your frustrations (Psalm 55:22) and give you the rest you need (Matthew 11:28). When the world is in turmoil, He is your shelter and safe place (Psalm 91:1–2), your unending source of strength and rock (Psalm 18:1–2). Nothing can separate you from the love of the Father, the Son, and the Holy Spirit that lives and loves inside you (Romans 8:38–39).

This world needs more of that kind of love. Love like that.

Loving God, I praise You for who You are: L-O-V-E. Your name is power and passion and patience and kindness and truth and protection and hope and perseverance. You never fail. Thank You for loving me.

JESUS IS
MY BROTHER

*Both the one who makes people holy and those who
are made holy are of the same family. So Jesus is
not ashamed to call them brothers and sisters.*
Hebrews 2:11–12 niv

Imagine the headline: Prince William, Prince of Wales, Announces Heroin Addict as Adopted Sibling and Coheir to the Crown. A shockingly unbelievable story like this could only appear on a parody news site or a grocery stand tabloid.

But consider a headline of the *true* story of your salvation: Jesus Christ, the King of Heaven's Only Son and Heir, Proclaims Filthy, Wretched Sinner as His Beloved Adopted Sister and Coheir to the Kingdom. This one is even *more* unbelievable.

Hebrews tell us that, despite our imperfection, Jesus

makes us holy. That's why He's not ashamed to call us His sisters. And not second-class sisters in name only. No, Christ Jesus is proud to share His inheritance with each of His siblings: salvation that provides eternal life in the Father's presence.

Don't get so comfortable in your salvation that you lose perspective on the awe factor of just how amazing your salvation is. Your today, tomorrow, and forever is secure—and glorious, not to mention totally awesome!

Jesus, I am proud and humbled to call You my brother. Thank You for claiming me as Your sister and making me holy. I don't deserve Your good gifts, but I am thankful for them. Amen.

MORE THAN WORDS

Truth, righteousness, peace, faith, and salvation are more than words. Learn how to apply them. You'll need them throughout your life. God's Word is an indispensable weapon.
EPHESIANS 6:13–17 MSG

Jesus died, just once, defeating death and ushering in our salvation and gift of grace. Because of what Jesus did on the cross, Satan will lose in the end. But until Jesus returns to earth, Satan's still playing his games. And we are his favorite toys.

God is our protector and doesn't ask us to initiate a battle against Satan (Exodus 14:14; Deuteronomy 3:22), but God does give us the tools we need to stand strong when we are attacked. The apostle Paul uses a powerful metaphor of a suit of armor in Ephesians 6, what's known as the Armor of God. Truth is a belt, holding our faith in place. Righteousness protects

our core, guarding our heart. Peace anchors our feet to the foundation upon which we stand. Our faith is a shield against the arrows that come out of nowhere. Our salvation is the crowning glory and work of Jesus, protecting us from the top down. And the Bible—our indispensable weapon against darkness—we can pick up like a sword and illuminate any situation with the light of God's wisdom.

God, thank You for arming me with the tools I need to stand strong, knowing You stand before me as my protector. I do not fear the battle I face today. Amen.

FINDING GOD IN LIFE'S STRUGGLES

And I want you to know, my dear brothers and sisters, that everything that has happened to me here has helped to spread the Good News. For everyone here, including the whole palace guard, knows that I am in chains because of Christ.

PHILIPPIANS 1:12–13 NLT

It's possible to welcome suffering into your life.

Are you kidding me? you're probably wondering. *Why would I do* that*?!*

The apostle Paul wrote his letter to the Philippians from behind the lock and key of a jail cell. It was just one of several times in his life when he was arrested or imprisoned for preaching the truth of Jesus. But his own suffering didn't come as a surprise to him. Jesus tells us in John 16, "Here on earth you will have

many trials and sorrows. But take heart, because I have overcome the world" (v. 33 NLT).

So, when difficult times come, find strength in the fact that no situation comes as a surprise to God. Look for His guiding hand. Ask for His intervention. Don't be afraid of tomorrow. Pray for His peace. Tap into real, lasting joy that's based on the goodness of God rather than on your circumstances. Find contentment in His love, a powerful force that remains no matter how difficult life gets. Finally, lean on Jesus, the Savior who has already conquered the darkness of the world for all time.

Jesus, I will welcome trials and
sorrows when they come. You have
already overcome them! Amen.

HIDDEN SINS

He said to me, "Son of man, have you seen what the elders of Israel are doing in the darkness, each at the shrine of his own idol? They say, 'The LORD does not see us; the LORD has forsaken the land.'"
 EZEKIEL 8:12 NIV

Time and again, God used Ezekiel's prophecies to tell the nation of Israel how furious He was with its idol worship. God's message for the leaders of Israel was clear: "Stop worshipping idols or suffer the consequences."

But idol worship continued—behind closed doors and in the dark. *If Ezekiel can't see it, he won't be able to tell the Lord.* Nice try, guys. Maybe they forgot that God is all-knowing (1 Chronicles 28:9) and always present (Jeremiah 23:23–24; Proverbs 15:3).

Turning off the lights to worship an idol seems like a ridiculous thing to do, but we are just as guilty of trying to hide our own sin. Maybe we think we can get

away with unseen sins like judging others, lust, envy, or pride. But God sees our hearts, and His Holy Spirit will convict us if we are tuned into His promptings.

Your Father God isn't a cosmic cop just waiting for you to mess up. He loves you and He wants the best for you. So let light flood the recesses of your heart and mind; ask Him to help you destroy those hidden sins.

Lord God, examine me, purify my heart,
and renew Your Holy Spirit in me. Amen.

HE REMAINS

You, Master, started it all, laid earth's foundations, then crafted the stars in the sky. Earth and sky will wear out, but not you; they become threadbare like an old coat; You'll fold them up like a worn-out cloak, and lay them away on the shelf. But you'll stay the same, year after year; you'll never fade, you'll never wear out.
HEBREWS 1:10–12 MSG

"You'll understand when you're older." Remember how that answer from a grown-up really burned you up? But as you grew older and matured, you *did* start to understand there are some things you simply can't explain to someone who hasn't experienced them personally.

The more we mature, the more we realize just how little we know—especially when we consider that God has no beginning and no end (Hebrews 7:3)—that He was the first and will be the last (Revelation 22:13). That He was the past, is the present, and will be the future. If

we spend too many minutes trying to find logic in such things, our little human brains might just melt. That's where faith steps in.

Within this puzzle of God's eternal nature comes comfort: God is always the same. He *never* changes. And that's true of His love for each of us. As long as God is, God is love.

Loving God, I praise You for Your constant nature. That forever fact about You brings me comfort, especially when my world is in flux. I love You, Father. Amen.

A PLAYGROUND BULLY

Don't be intimidated in any way by your enemies. This will be a sign to them that they are going to be destroyed, but that you are going to be saved, even by God himself.
PHILIPPIANS 1:28 NLT

Let's call Satan what he is: a playground bully.

Playground bullies are manipulators. Some days they may seem harmless enough, but that's when they're scanning the schoolyard for weaknesses in other kids to pounce on. They plant fear in minds and hearts by their threats, physicality, torments, and insults. But it's not what they can *do* that has any power (because playground bullies aren't in charge—adults are), it's the mental games they play that put lasting fearful thoughts inside other kids—and that fear can grow to

be crippling for the child.

So when you feel the world's playground bully circling, take advice from the apostle Paul: don't be intimidated. Stand tall and confident in the knowledge that Satan's days are numbered, and he knows it. Ask the Holy Spirit to guard your heart from the lies of manipulation Satan whispers into your ear. Jesus is your friend, and He is near. He's the one who defeated Satan, sin, and all the evil of the world once and for all time.

Today I refuse to be intimidated by my enemies, Lord. You are my daily, minute-to-minute Savior who can and will save me from any situation. Thank You.

LORD, PLEASE BE GENTLE

I know, Lord, that our lives are not our own.
We are not able to plan our own course.
So correct me, Lord, but please be gentle.
JEREMIAH 10:23–24 NLT

We map out our route by filling up planners and calendars. We place firm but gentle grips at 10 and 2 o'clock on the steering wheel of our lives. We merge lanes as we set goals and take steps necessary to accomplish them. And then a humongous deer of a crisis bounds out of the woods into our path and we realize—in one terrifying moment—that we don't have the control over our lives we think we do.

God's expert ability to plan our lives is so much better than ours, but it's often terrifying to give up that control. Jesus, in the garden of Gethsemane just hours

before His arrest, trial, and crucifixion, admitted His own desire to alter God's plans when He prayed, "If it is possible, let this cup of suffering be taken away from me." But even in His struggle, He knew God's way was ultimately the best, most perfect way when He set aside His pride and earnestly prayed, "Yet I want your will to be done, not mine" (Matthew 26:39 NLT).

"Your will, not mine" is a powerful and often scary prayer to pray. Just remember God's great love for you. Don't be afraid to ask and accept His gentle correction to your course.

Father, take control. But please be gentle. Amen.

LET LOVE PROSPER

Love prospers when a fault is forgiven,
but dwelling on it separates close friends.
PROVERBS 17:9 NLT

Forgive and forget. Sounds simple, right?

If only it *were* simple. But that would take short memories and humility instead of our elephant-like rememberers and out-of-control egos.

So how can you truly forgive and forget? First, realize that real, lasting, healing forgiveness is something that comes from God. Ask the Holy Spirit to help you get a handle on it. Acknowledge how difficult forgiveness is, and thank Him for forgiving your sins over and over again.

Next, understand the difference between *forgetting* and *choosing to not remember*. God doesn't ask you to develop amnesia; wrongs done to you will always be a part of your story. But when God forgives you,

He banishes your wrongs from His thoughts, as He explains in Isaiah 43:25 NLT: "I—yes, I alone—will blot out your sins for my own sake and will never think of them again." And the psalmist wrote that God "has removed our sins as far from us as the east is from the west" (Psalm 103:12 NLT). So as the forgiver, you must do the same for the forgivee.

God can and will use difficult points in a relationship to create fertile ground for forgiveness. As Proverbs 17:9 promises, love will then prosper and grow.

Forgiving Father, You know how difficult it is for me to forgive sometimes. Help me create a fertile ground of pardon so that love can grow. Amen.

PRESS AHEAD

I focus on this one thing: Forgetting the past and looking forward to what lies ahead, I press on to reach the end of the race and receive the heavenly prize for which God, through Christ Jesus, is calling us.
PHILIPPIANS 3:13–14 NLT

"It's called a yoga *practice*—not a yoga *perfect*!"

If you've ever taken a yoga class, perhaps you've heard the instructor say something like this. Every journey, every growth opportunity takes perseverance. It takes the willingness to press ahead and to forge through failure.

In Philippians, Paul describes the Christian life as a foot race, and he may have understood this metaphor better than most. Paul had good reason to want to forget his past. This former persecutor of Christians held the coats of those who stoned Stephen, the first Christian martyr (Acts 7:57–58). We have all done things for which

we are ashamed, and we live in the tension of what we have been and what we want to be. But the fact remains that our hope is in Christ, and because of that we can let go of guilt and celebrate our newness in Him.

Today, don't relive your past. Instead, focus on deepening your relationship with God now. Thank Him for His forgiveness and then move on to a life of greater and unshakable faith and obedience. You can look forward to tomorrow.

Father, help me to let go of my past so I can focus on what's ahead: a glorious present and future with You!

REPLACING WORRY

Don't fret or worry. Instead of worrying, pray.
Let petitions and praises shape your worries into
prayers, letting God know your concerns. Before
you know it, a sense of God's wholeness, everything
coming together for good, will come and settle you
down. It's wonderful what happens when Christ
displaces worry at the center of your life.

PHILIPPIANS 4:6–7 MSG

Has worry made a home in your heart? Are you so used to stomach-knotting fretting tied to anxious thoughts that getting rid of it seems impossible? Are you concerned that if you extracted worry from your life it may actually leave a hole in your heart?

Our Father, in His unending compassion for our hearts and spirits, gives us a perfect replacement for worry: prayer.

When you replace worry with prayer, God's Word

promises us not just an absence of anxiety and fear but the *addition* of peace. Telling Him about your concerns brings the peace of Christ that goes beyond any understanding or rational explanation. Praising Him for what He has done in the past and clinging to the hope of what He's doing now and in your future brings wholeness that can only come from God's perfect plan. Prayer brings rest, contentment, safety, security, and confidence only found in the Savior, Jesus Christ.

Want to worry less? Then pray more!

Worry has no home in this heart anymore, Father. Take away my anxious thoughts and assure me that You are near. When worries try to creep back, replace them with the peace of Christ.

KEEP YOUR GUARD UP

About an hour later, someone else spoke up, really adamant: "He's got to have been with him! He's got 'Galilean' written all over him." Peter said, "Man, I don't know what you're talking about." At that very moment, the last word hardly off his lips, a rooster crowed.
LUKE 22:59–60 MSG

The rooster's crow may have been the worst "aha" moment of Peter's life. After being so amped up for the cause of Christ that he told Jesus he was ready to go with Him "to prison and to death" (Luke 22:33 ESV), the very next day Peter denied even *knowing* Jesus.

Oh "how the mighty have fallen" (2 Samuel 1:27 ESV).

We, like Peter, are vulnerable to temptation—especially during times of great stress. Hard lines we've set for ourselves get blurry as we struggle through difficulties. But, when in the Garden of Gethsemane, Jesus gave us an example of what to do to resist:

1. Pray (Mark 14:35).

2. Seek support of others (Mark 14:33, 37, 40, 41).

3. Focus on God's purpose for you (Mark 14:36).

Peter's story doesn't end at the rooster crow. He found redemption and forgiveness through Jesus and went on to do mighty works in forming the early church. Don't let your failures define you either. God can and will use a willing and humble heart for great things.

Jesus, create in me a pure heart that resists temptation. I'm living for You and You only! Amen.

ANTICIPATE HIS MIGHTY WORKS

O Lord, if you heal me, I will be truly healed;
if you save me, I will be truly saved.
My praises are for you alone!
JEREMIAH 17:14 NLT

What tops your list of prayer requests today? What relationship are you asking God to repair, sickness to remedy, need to meet, or circumstance to change?

It takes an incredible amount of humility to approach the throne of the King of heaven and boldly ask for. . . anything. But the truth is that we don't have to wonder *if* He will act, because scripture tells us: "This is the confidence we have in approaching God: that if we ask anything according to his will, he hears us. And if we know that he hears us—whatever we ask—we know that we have what we asked of him" (1 John 5:14–15 NIV).

Whatever need is on your heart, your loving Father invites you to lay it at His feet and know He will meet that need. When your heart is aligned with His, your desires will be in harmony with His plans. He will act according to His will—in a mighty, perfect, and powerful way!

*God, I need You to step in and take control of this.
I am struggling, and I need something to change.
If You choose to bring change, I know You will
make something beautiful and whole and perfect.
I praise You for Your good and perfect will for my life.*

ROOTED

*Let your roots grow down into him, and let
your lives be built on him. Then your faith
will grow strong in the truth you were taught,
and you will overflow with thankfulness.*
COLOSSIANS 2:7 NLT

There are few attributes more admirable in another person than a strong faith. Faith-filled individuals appear to have an inner strength that can stand in the face of any trial. They have a faith that seems to grow stronger even as their world crumbles around them.

How can this be? Their faith is rooted in Christ.

In Colossians 2, Paul uses a word picture that describes Christians as trees. These plants take nutrients from the soil through their roots, just as we take our life-giving strength from Christ. The more and longer we draw our strength from Him, the stronger our faith will grow and thrive.

How do we grow a stronger faith that's deeply rooted in Jesus?

- Read and study the Word of God (Romans 10:17).

- Pray (Hebrews 4:14–16).

- Do life with other people of faith (Proverbs 13:10).

- Trust God—especially in the difficulties of life (2 Corinthians 1:9).

- Thank and praise Him (Hebrews 13:15–16).

Father, grow my roots deep into the foundation of Your Son. I want to be that person who is immovable even when the wind and storms of life trials beat against me. Help me to stand tall and be an example to others of Your true, steadfast, unshakable nature. Amen.

SOLID FOOD

You are like babies who need milk and cannot eat solid food. For someone who lives on milk is still an infant and doesn't know how to do what is right. Solid food is for those who are mature, who through training have the skill to recognize the difference between right and wrong.

HEBREWS 5:12–14 NLT

It's a fun and messy milestone in a baby's development when she starts learning to eat solid food. And just like everything in an infant's life, trying new textures and tastes and using a spoon and a sippy cup take practice.

But with patience and encouragement from Mom and Dad, most developing children *do* move from milk or formula to rice cereal to mashed bananas to steak.

So when the writer of Hebrews chastises the church for remaining immature in its faith, it's a significant matter. To grow, the church needs someone to reteach

its people the basics, feeding them the milk of God's Word. As they then put into practice what they learn, their capacity to understand more will grow. They'll gain the skill to tell right from wrong.

No matter where you are on the milk-to-solid-food spectrum, there's always room to grow. If you're comfortable with your bottle, you're missing out on the delicacies God offers as His banquet feast for His beloved children. What's holding you back?

Father, give me a hunger for You, so my palate can mature, and I can enjoy Your gifts and work more effectively for Your glory. Amen.

TOO MUCH TALK

*Too much talk leads to sin. Be sensible
and keep your mouth shut.*
PROVERBS 10:19 NLT

Our days are filled with talk. Face-to-face, on the phone, over email, through texts, on social media. Sometimes we may feel like it's impossible to stop words from gushing out—*especially* when we have strong feelings about what we're saying.

But unfiltered talk leaves us feeling unsteady, disrupted, back on our heels, and more likely to hurt someone else. It's not the wisest way to use our words.

When your words veer out of control, shut your mouth. Simple enough, but oh, so difficult! Scripture explains in James 3 that shutting up is the best option because "no human being can tame the tongue. It is a restless evil, full of deadly poison" (v. 8 NIV). The Psalmist knew he needed help with this when he

prayed, "Set a guard over my mouth, LORD; keep watch over the door of my lips" (141:3 NIV).

But God isn't asking us to walk this earth as mute women who *never* speak. True, godly wisdom means our words are thoughtful, prayerful, and measured. They are considerate, encouraging, and helpful. Today, ask God to fill your mouth with His words and the wisdom to know when to speak so that your words are "always full of grace, seasoned with salt" (Colossians 4:6 NIV).

*God, be the Lord and gatekeeper of my
words. With guidance from Your Spirit,
I will stop and think before I plow on.*

ALWAYS A BEST MAN

*"He must become greater and greater,
and I must become less and less."*
JOHN 3:30 NLT

Jesus' cousin John dunked converts in the Jordan River in preparation for Jesus' arrival. This ministry had resulted in John's own followers, as well as rumors that *he* was actually the long-awaited Messiah.

John must've been tempted to use his reputation for personal gain. Whether it was offers of financial bribes for salvation or invitations to prestigious parties, scripture tells us John the Baptist remained humble and committed to the singular calling on his life. He even told his followers that he considered the joy he felt at the arrival of Jesus to be like that of a best man on his best friend's wedding day (John 3:29).

What was John's secret to such humility? God had given him a heart for the Messiah—an uncanny

understanding of the hope Christ's salvation would bring to the world. John was tapped into the power of God, and nothing would distract his focus.

What about you? What singular calling has God placed on your life? Ask Him to make that calling clear and to show you how amid your ministry—and life— Jesus will become greater and you less.

Father, may the love of Jesus overtake my thoughts, actions, and speech in everything so that my circle no longer sees me—but a beautiful reflection of You.

THAT NEW COVENANT SMELL

The old system under the law of Moses was only a shadow, a dim preview of the good things to come, not the good things themselves. The sacrifices under that system were repeated again and again, year after year, but they were never able to provide perfect cleansing for those who came to worship.

HEBREWS 10:1 NLT

Sometimes it's good to do with what we already have. Maybe it's not the newest, shiniest, or fanciest thing around, but it works well enough (mostly), and we can get by.

But when we're talking about the old covenant (priests and sacrifices and atonement and ceremonial washing and more) in contrast to the new covenant, there's no comparing the two. The writer of Hebrews

describes the old way as "only a shadow, a dim preview of the good things to come." The heroes of the faith (mentioned in Hebrews 11) from the old covenant accepted and lived within the law and got a small taste of God's glory. But we who live under the new covenant can receive the perfect cleansing that Jesus' sacrifice on the cross gives us.

God offers you the best, the most perfect new life you can never hope to earn on your own. Don't make do with what you already have when it comes to your faith. Accept God's grace, His cleansing, and His new mercies every day (Lamentations 3:23).

New Covenant God, thank You for making
a new way—the best way—Jesus. Amen.

PASS IT ON!

Let the message about Christ, in all its richness, fill your lives. Teach and counsel each other with all the wisdom he gives. Sing psalms and hymns and spiritual songs to God with thankful hearts.
COLOSSIANS 3:16 NLT

What have you learned about Jesus lately? Maybe you've been blessed by something you read in scripture. Have you received an answer to prayer? Perhaps you've heard a song lyric that touched your heart.

Whatever you're learning, don't keep it to yourself. Share it with others! Jesus explains why in Matthew 5:14–16 MSG: "You're here to be light, bringing out the God-colors in the world. God is not a secret to be kept. . . . If I make you light-bearers, you don't think I'm going to hide you under a bucket, do you? I'm putting you on a light stand. Now that I've put you there on a hilltop, on a light stand—shine! . . . By opening up to

others, you'll prompt people to open up with God."

Talk about what you've learned in conversation, send a text, post it on social media. Sound scary? Your personal experience doesn't have to be awkward or off-putting. You don't have to be a Bible scholar to share what Jesus means to you and what He's doing in your life. You never know when your story is just what someone else needs to hear.

Jesus, show me ways to share You more intentionally. Help my story encourage others to experience You more fully.

JUST A FEW

A truly wise person uses few words.
PROVERBS 17:27 NLT

Women talk more than men: fact or fiction?

Despite your own opinion about this statement, researchers are divided on whether it's true and whether there's a biological reason one way or the other. Regardless of whether we're the chatty sort or generally quiet, scripture is clear: to be wise, talk less.

So why are few words better than a whole slew? Consider:

1. It's impossible to listen while talking. "Understand this, my dear brothers and sisters: You must all be quick to listen, slow to speak, and slow to get angry" (James 1:19 NLT).

2. Truly listening results in more thoughtful replies. "There is more hope for a fool than for someone

who speaks without thinking" (Proverbs 29:20 NLT).

3. Speaking fewer words can give each one more importance, and you'll likely choose them more carefully. "Let everything you say be good and helpful, so that your words will be an encouragement to those who hear them" (Ephesians 4:29 NLT).

You know the difference between idle chatter and meaningful conversation. When you hear yourself talking just for talking's sake, take a breath and listen. Without the noise of your own voice, you may just hear God speak in a new and active way!

God, teach me the discipline of listening and thinking before I speak. Give me the right words that are filled with Your truth. Amen.

PATIENT ENDURANCE

Patient endurance is what you need now,
so that you will continue to do God's will.
Then you will receive all that he has promised.
Hebrews 10:36 nlt

Patience is a word often associated with waiting—in a line, in a reception area, for a special day on the calendar, for a loved one's arrival. And when a mom instructs a child to be patient, she's probably asking her to be still and quiet while she waits.

Endurance is a word often used to describe what it takes to be a long-distance runner. It connotes grueling, unrelenting work toward a goal, coupled with a runner's confidence of completing that goal and the hope of a race well run.

Hebrews 10:36 urges us believers to practice *patient endurance* as we do God's will then wait to receive all that God has promised. To do so quietly while

unrelentingly working toward our goal. We can do that by expecting God to move according to His timing. To anticipate receiving all He has promised as we do His will. That means to get busy, to endure, and endeavor to do God's work where we are, with the unique abilities and passions with which He's gifted us, using them to love God and others (Mark 12:30–31).

Father, I admit I struggle with patience.
My head knows Your timing is perfect,
but my selfish heart wants everything
You've promised NOW. Give me good work
to do as I strive toward the goal. Amen.

YOU WILL
BE CHANGED

*"The Spirit of the L*ORD *will come powerfully*
upon you, and you will prophesy with them;
and you will be changed into a different person.
Once these signs are fulfilled, do whatever
your hand finds to do, for God is with you."
1 SAMUEL 10:6–7 NIV

We often associate heart transformation with the New Testament—from John the Baptist blazing the trail to repentance (Matthew 3) to Paul's assurance that we are made into new creatures in Christ (2 Corinthians 5:17). But throughout history, God has delighted in radical transformation.

Consider the account of Samuel anointing Saul as king. First God gave Saul a new heart (1 Samuel 10:9). Then, generations before the Holy Spirit arrived at

Pentecost (Acts 2), the Spirit came powerfully on Saul and changed him—into a different person (1 Samuel 10:10)!

This same transformation is available to you today, sister! Is your heart heavy with worry, jealousy, self-loathing, or hatred? If so, release your heart to God who has a new one ready, just for you. All you need to do is pray, asking God to take away your old heart. He's merely waiting for you to sign the release forms required for the spiritual transplant.

God, I release my stained heart to You.
Please replace it with Your pure heart and
change me in a radical way. I can't do this
on my own. For only You can make lasting,
real, holy, perfect change in me. Amen.

OPPORTUNITIES ABOUND

*Live wisely among those who are not believers,
and make the most of every opportunity. Let your
conversation be gracious and attractive so that
you will have the right response for everyone.*
COLOSSIANS 4:5–6 NLT

Every day brings new opportunities to speak God's loving truth to the people around us. Almost every interaction, in fact, is a chance to offer encouragement. To spread some joy. To lighten a load. To be Jesus to someone who desperately needs Him. "God has given us the task of telling everyone what he is doing," Paul explains in 2 Corinthians 5:20 (MSG). "We're Christ's representatives."

Yet most days we don't even *see* these opportunities, let alone *act* on them. Why? It's not because we don't

want to make the most of every opportunity. It's not because we don't care about others. It's because we're distracted by ourselves: *our* to-do list, *our* needs and desires, and *our* thoughts.

So how can you change your mindset to take advantage of these opportunities? Start your day by reviewing your calendar and pray for the individuals you'll be in contact with today. Open yourself to the possibility of unexpected opportunities as well. Ask the Holy Spirit to fill your words with grace, calm, love, and respect for others. Your Spirit-led love can plant a seed that may grow roots of a deep faith.

God, show me how to love the hearts of the people around me. I want to make the most of every opportunity to spread Your loving-kindness.

OPINIONS:
WE'VE GOT 'EM

*An unfriendly person pursues selfish ends and
against all sound judgment starts quarrels.
Fools find no pleasure in understanding but
delight in airing their own opinions.*
PROVERBS 18:1–2 NIV

If you'd like to know someone's opinion about anything, hop over to her social media page, and odds are good you'll see what she thinks. Whether it's a post about what the government is doing right/wrong or a link to a news article or a pithy quote that supports/refutes a specific view, social media has given the masses a platform to opinionate for the world to see.

While it's not wrong to have an opinion that's grounded in God's truth, Proverbs 18:1–2 encourages us to set our own feelings aside to first care about the

other person and put in the time and effort to understand him or her, asking God for wisdom in the situation (see James 1:5–6). That means seeing others through God's eyes—as deeply loved and highly valued people.

We should strive to first and foremost be known as women of love and understanding—not recognized for our knee-jerk reactions and loud opinions. When others know us as a listening ear, they'll be more likely to ask our opinions, opening the opportunity for us to share the love of Christ in every situation.

Father, when my own ball of feelings and opinions wells up inside me, don't let it drown out the voice of the Holy Spirit. He is who I want to follow. Amen.

MICHAL'S MISSTEP

*As the ark of the Lord was entering the City of David,
Michal daughter of Saul watched from a window.
And when she saw King David leaping and dancing
before the Lord, she despised him in her heart.*
2 Samuel 6:16 niv

Scripture doesn't tell us exactly what Michal's problem was, but it's likely this contempt for her husband, David, didn't start when she looked out her window and saw his passionate, animated worship before the Lord.

Perhaps she thought it was undignified for a king to display such emotion. Or maybe she thought celebration was a trivial pursuit as there were more pressing matters in the kingdom. Whatever the reason, Michal's ongoing bitterness and resentment escalated into a fight (2 Samuel 6:20–23) that did real damage to their relationship, resulting in their childless marriage.

Bitterness and resentment are insidious emotions that may simmer on the back burner of a relationship for some time before coming to a boil. But bitterness has no power to change circumstances, and resentment only makes a bad situation worse. Left unchecked, they can destroy a relationship. Although you may not have control over what happens to you, you *do* control how you respond. When you feel those simmering emotions, reset, ask God for clarity, and deal with your feelings.

God, I cannot live with this bitterness
in my heart. Cleanse me and give me a
new heart full of love and patience.

A GOD WHO BENDS DOWN

Bend down, O Lord, and hear my prayer;
answer me, for I need your help.

PSALM 86:1 NLT

Preschool teachers spend much of their days down on the level of their students. Kneeling to tie a shoe, sitting on tiny chairs at miniature tables, and bending to hear a soft voice or offer a hug. Sometimes they lower themselves for practical reasons, but other times they get down simply to show these little people that they are important, valued, and loved.

The writer of Psalms asked God to bend down, to listen to his prayer for help—a brazen request to the almighty Creator of the sky and sea! But God heard that request, just as He hears your requests today. Jesus proved once and for all that the Lord is a God who gets

down on the level of His children. He came to earth fully God and fully human, bending low to pull us out of the pit of sin. Jesus knows bending down—low enough to sacrifice His life on the cross.

Yes, God will bend down to look you in the eye, to hear your whispered need, but He won't stay bent over. He'll pick you up in His strong arms and take you to where you can weather the storms of life.

Father, I need You. Please bend down so
I can see You and feel Your presence here
as I whisper my fears into Your ear.
You alone can rescue me. Amen.

A SATISFYING MEAL

Jesus said to them, "My food is to do the will of him who sent me and to accomplish his work."

JOHN 4:34 ESV

Have you ever been so focused on a project that tasks like drinking water, sleeping, or even eating get pushed to the very bottom of your to-do list? If you're passionate and excited about what you're doing, time has a way of slip-sliding past.

The disciples had been with Jesus long enough by now to know that when it came to loving others, He was always in that deep-focus mode. So they'd gotten into the habit of gently reminding Him, "Rabbi, eat" (John 4:31 ESV).

Although Jesus absolutely needed to nourish His human body, He also understood the fulfillment that comes from doing God's will—the kind of satisfaction that leaves your soul full after a filling, spiritual

feast. Maybe you've experienced that fulfillment too—in leading someone to Christ, doing someone a kindness, or using your God-given talents to further His kingdom.

God has uniquely positioned you at His banquet table with a deeply satisfying feast laid before you. If you don't recognize what or where your soul food is, ask Him to show you. Then be on the lookout for the opportunity to dive in, heart first.

Father, I long for that deep satisfaction that I only find in working for You. My napkin is laid in my lap. I'm ready for the first course. Amen.

GOD'S APPROVED MESSENGERS

*For we speak as messengers approved by
God to be entrusted with the Good News.
Our purpose is to please God, not people.
He alone examines the motives of our hearts.*

1 Thessalonians 2:4 nlt

"Don't forget: You're representing our family." As children grow and become more independent, parents send them out into the world—often with this reminder. Do you remember what it was like to realize that your actions reflected more than just yourself? Maybe you've more recently been on the parent side of this scenario, cautiously hoping your kid makes the best choices.

God entrusts us—His children—with His message of love for the world. We don't have to be preachers

or pastors or have degrees in theology. His commands are simple: Love God; love others. We are His approved representatives, given freedom to share Jesus through our actions and words. What does that look like in everyday life? Begin your day in praise of the one who loves you so much that He gave up His only Son on the cross. Then let that praise inhabit the rest of your day. Share with others what God is doing in your life. When you realize the abundantly loving way God interacts with you, you'll want to let love rule your actions and interactions as well.

I'm Your messenger, Father. Make me worthy of such a calling. Make my daily life a story of You that clearly communicates Your love, Your grace, Your strength, and Your salvation.

FORWARD THINKERS

All these people were still living by faith when they died. They did not receive the things promised; they only saw them and welcomed them from a distance, admitting that they were foreigners and strangers on earth.

HEBREWS 11:13 NIV

Each family tree has its own unique story, but every family has a heritage passed down from one generation to the next.

The heritage of faith in God's family tree is a line that goes back to creation. From Adam and Eve in the garden through the single righteous family of Noah to Abraham and Sarah, Isaac and Jacob, Hebrews 11:13 tells us these individuals did not receive the promised salvation while on earth, but they never lost hope that God would provide a way for them to be with Him.

If you're going through a difficult time, God's

promises may seem far away. Don't give up! Take courage from these heroes of faith who lived and died without seeing the reward of their belief on earth but who are now at home in God's presence. Ask God to show you what He has promised from afar—even a glimpse of what's to come can help you stand strong.

God, I know this place is not my home, and I'm trying to keep that in perspective as I grow more and more homesick to be with You. Thank You for the heritage of faith in Your family tree. I am blessed to be a part of it. Amen.

REFRESHING GENEROSITY

Give freely and become more wealthy;
be stingy and lose everything.
The generous will prosper; those who
refresh others will themselves be refreshed.

PROVERBS 11:24–25 NLT

In our efforts to be safe and secure, there's a temptation to hold on to wealth. When we feel unsafe, threatened, or unbalanced, it's human nature to want to insulate ourselves from possible (or inevitable) disaster. To hoard. To keep more than we need. Money can give us a blissful (although false) sense that we can handle any calamity that comes.

In these verses in Proverbs, we see a paradox: we become richer by being generous. The world says to hold on to as much as possible. But God blesses those

who give freely of their possessions, time, and energy. When we give, God supplies us with more so that we can give more. God enriches the lives of the generous with a sense of peace about money and things. Giving also helps us gain a correct perspective on our possessions. We realize they were never ours to begin with; God blesses us with possessions that can be used to help others. What then do we gain by giving? Freedom from enslavement to our possessions, the joy of helping others, and God's approval.

Generous and giving God, I have so much to thank You for. Show me what You want me to do with my time, my possessions, and my finances. Give me a heart that is free and ready to give. Remind me that my strength lies in You alone.

SOMETHING BETTER

These were all commended for their faith, yet none of them received what had been promised, since God had planned something better for us so that only together with us would they be made perfect.
HEBREWS 11:39–40 NIV

God created us for community. Jesus established His church to be individuals who make up one unit. And the apostle Paul described the church as a single body with many parts (1 Corinthians 12), each part dependent on the other parts to be whole. We often think about this passage in the context of our own church congregations or believers all over the planet, but it's bigger than that.

Hebrews 11:39–40 explains that God gives unity among believers throughout history. All of God's children—since day one of creation—will be glorified together. Not only are we one in the body of Christ

with living believers, but we are also one with all those who ever lived. It takes all of us along with Jesus to be perfect in Him.

Your faith stands on the shoulders of history. You are counted alongside the names of the Hebrews 11 faith hall of fame, the faithful of today, and the generations of believers to arrive before Christ's return.

God, I am thankful to be a part of the body of Christ. Give me a heart for Your community. May I never take my role for granted. Amen.

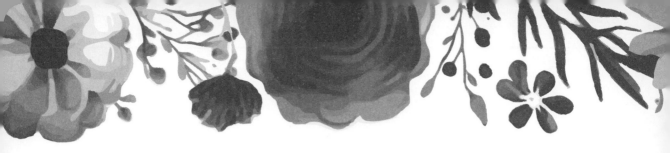

NOT A GHOST

"Why are you troubled, and why do doubts rise in your minds? Look at my hands and my feet. It is I myself! Touch me and see; a ghost does not have flesh and bones, as you see I have."

LUKE 24:38–40 NIV

When Jesus came back to life in the tomb, He may have wondered if He'd just awoken from a nightmare. Perhaps His first physical sensations were the gaping nail holes in His hands and feet, verifying it'd all really happened. He'd been crucified, and resurrection power had brought Him back to life!

So when the newly risen Lord's friends reacted to Him with eyes wide with terror, Jesus gave them the simplest and most compelling evidence He could: "Look, touch—I'm real. I'm not a ghost!" Still, Luke wrote, it wasn't until Jesus "opened their minds so they could understand the Scriptures" and His title role in

them that the disciples started to grasp their new reality (24:45–48 NIV).

Following Christ sometimes means you don't have all the *why* and *how* answers to your questions. Scripture tells you that living a life of faith requires setting aside your human desire to understand the whole picture (see 2 Corinthians 5:7; Hebrews 11). But while Jesus, in His newly risen body, isn't here with you today, He *will* give you clarity and insight through His Word if you continually seek Him there.

Jesus, give me a hunger for Your Word and clarity from its living, powerful message. Amen.

GOD'S GOOD CHOICE

God chose to save us through our Lord Jesus Christ, not to pour out his anger on us. Christ died for us so that, whether we are dead or alive when he returns, we can live with him forever.
1 Thessalonians 5:9–10 nlt

There's freedom in making a choice. A choice gives us a voice in a vote, allows us to follow our conscience. Decisions bring about empowerment in our own circumstances.

God, in His great love and compassion for us, *made the choice* to send Jesus to save us from our sins. No other authority told Him that's the way it had to be. He was not bound by a legal agreement or forced to act a certain way. He wasn't tricked or coerced. *He chose to save us.* The same is true for our Savior Jesus. "No one can take my life from me. I sacrifice it voluntarily," He explained in John 10:18 (nlt). "For I have the authority

to lay it down when I want to and also to take it up again. For this is what my Father has commanded."

Today, thank Jesus for choosing to follow the perfect will of God, who chose to make a way for us, His children, to be with Him forever. Knowing that, I can choose to be unshakable.

Father, You demonstrated once and for all that You love the world so much that You gave up Your Son. Thank You for choosing me. Amen.

ROOTED AND SECURE

Wickedness never brings stability,
but the godly have deep roots.
PROVERBS 12:3 NLT

Sin never brings security.

This may seem like an obvious statement, but we've each fallen into the trap of using deceit to try to steady our out-of-control world. *What he doesn't know won't hurt him,* we think of a lie of omission. *I'd never normally* [fill in the blank], *and I know it's wrong. . .but it'll help me out of this jam and I'll never do it again!*

This kind of thinking may give us a false sense of security and control, but the wisdom in Proverbs 12:19 tells us, "Truth lasts; lies are here today, gone tomorrow" (MSG).

Real, forever stability and peace come from a living

relationship with our Father God. Jeremiah 17:7–8 (NLT) paints a beautiful word picture of that life:

> *"But blessed are those who trust in the LORD and have made the LORD their hope and confidence. They are like trees planted along a riverbank, with roots that reach deep into the water. Such trees are not bothered by the heat or worried by long months of drought. Their leaves stay green, and they never stop producing fruit."*

When we put our hope in God, we're trusting Him to take care of our needs—big and small (Matthew 6:26). We're secure, knowing He loves us and will protect us (Isaiah 41:10). Are you looking for stability today? Get rooted in His truth!

Father, today I choose to put my hope in You.

LIFE'S A GARDEN

*Work at living in peace with everyone,
and work at living a holy life. . . . Watch out
that no poisonous root of bitterness grows
up to trouble you, corrupting many.*
HEBREWS 12:14–15 NLT

Gardeners learn it's easier to pull up small weeds before the roots have a chance to develop, so they're on constant watch for the beginnings of weeds to pull and destroy. It's hard work, but the rewards of a bountiful harvest are worth it.

Hebrews describes bitterness in a relationship as a "poisonous root"—a slow-growing weed. It starts out as nothing: a little annoyance or an unintentional slight. But if we're not on guard, a seed of bitterness can find a crack in our hearts where it burrows in and sprouts.

If you find yourself in a state of annoyance with

someone, if you're rolling your eyes in her presence, if you find yourself avoiding her, check your heart. Has a bitter root sprouted? Get out the gardening gloves and pull and dig to remove and destroy that root!

A right relationship with God leads to right relationships with others. Although we will not always feel loving toward all other people, we must pursue peace as we become more like Jesus.

God, I know what it feels like when a bitter root has developed in my heart—and I choose peace! Show me where I need to dig. Amen.

WORTHY OF HIS CALL

So we keep on praying for you, asking our God to enable you to live a life worthy of his call. May he give you the power to accomplish all the good things your faith prompts you to do. Then the name of our Lord Jesus will be honored because of the way you live, and you will be honored along with him.

2 Thessalonians 1:11–12 NLT

What is God's calling on your life?

That may seem like a big, loaded question. While we're each created with unique gifts (Romans 12:6), we each have the free will to make decisions for ourselves within the will of God. So, as Christians, our calling from God is to become like Christ. Romans 8:29 says, "For God knew his people in advance, and he chose them to become like his Son, so that his Son would be the firstborn among many brothers and sisters" (NLT).

Becoming Christlike is a gradual, lifelong process

that will be completed when we see Christ face-to-face (1 John 3:2). To be "worthy" of this calling means to want to do what is right and good—to model our lives after Jesus by loving God and loving others. Not one of us is perfect yet, but we're moving in that direction as Christ and His power work in us every day.

Father, I am worthy of Your plan for my life because You make me worthy. Lead me in the lifelong process of becoming more and more like Jesus.

BRING IT ON

So we say with confidence, "The Lord
is my helper; I will not be afraid.
What can mere mortals do to me?"
Hebrews 13:6 niv

The cares, worries, challenges, and frustrations of dealing with difficult people have an uncanny way of distracting us from the fact that if we're in God's family we've *already* triumphed over every challenge someone can throw at us. We have nothing to fear. We're saved. We are victorious. God wins!

But life happens—twenty-four hours a day, seven days a week. Seasons of discouragement, setbacks, and disappointments shift our focus away from the truth of our situation. People fail us; some may even attack our faith. Instead of looking to the Light, we turn around, distracted by the isolating darkness that sets fear in our hearts.

Before these times come (and they come for us all), arm yourself with this mighty reminder from Hebrews 13:6 (a.k.a. Psalm 118:6). Make it your heart's battle cry in the face of every difficult person: "God is my confidence! I will not fear because He is *already* helping me. Do your worst, world, because He is bigger!"

Believe it, sister. He's got your back—now live like it!

Father, I need Your help today. My spirit is beat up by the constant barrage of challenges from difficult people. Restore my spirit of power, love, and mental strength that You have promised me (2 Timothy 1:7).

A WAKE-UP CALL

My dear child, don't shrug off God's discipline, but don't be crushed by it either. It's the child he loves that he disciplines; the child he embraces, he also corrects.

HEBREWS 12:5–6 MSG

From the time a child is old enough to understand right and wrong, a loving parent will correct her wayward behavior. Although it's uncomfortable for parent and child alike, the cost of *not* disciplining is far greater than the parent doling out and the child enduring correction.

As adults, we probably don't receive the same kind of discipline from our parents or other authority figures on a regular basis. But no matter how old we are, God *does* discipline us when we're outside of His perfect plan for our lives.

Hebrews urges us to listen to God's correction, accept it, adjust, and understand that we're being

corrected because He loves us and wants the best for us. Hebrews 12:11 provides a dose of reality followed by a great promise: "No discipline is enjoyable while it is happening—it's painful! But afterward there will be a peaceful harvest of right living for those who are trained in this way" (NLT).

Be willing to endure God's discipline, knowing a peaceful harvest of right living will follow. Remember, God's way is always the best way.

Good Father, please help me understand that Your discipline is guiding me back to Your good and righteous path for my life. Despite my actions, that's the path I want to be on. Amen.

THE LOVE OF GOD

May the Lord lead your hearts into a full understanding and expression of the love of God and the patient endurance that comes from Christ.
2 Thessalonians 3:5 NLT

God loves you.

Maybe you've known this since you were a tiny child, but despite its simplicity, God's love is so vast—so wonderfully mysterious—that it'll take a lifetime (plus eternity) to understand it fully.

Today, meditate on these truths so you can understand better God's almighty love for you:

- "The Lord is compassionate and merciful, slow to get angry and filled with unfailing love" (Psalm 103:8 NLT).

- "He heals the brokenhearted and bandages their wounds" (Psalm 147:3 NLT).

- "Nothing in all creation will ever be able to separate us from the love of God" (Romans 8:39 NLT).

- "For this is how God loved the world: He gave his one and only Son, so that everyone who believes in him will not perish but have eternal life" (John 3:16 NLT).

- "But God is so rich in mercy, and he loved us so much, that even though we were dead because of our sins, he gave us life when he raised Christ from the dead" (Ephesians 2:4–5 NLT).

There is no better place for you to be and no more secure situation than resting in the love of God. When all else fails. . .His love is *more* than enough.

God, teach me to understand Your love more fully so that I can show that powerful love to others. Amen.

A PRIZED POSSESSION

*He chose to give birth to us by giving us
his true word. And we, out of all creation,
became his prized possession.*
JAMES 1:18 NLT

Out of everything God created—the majestic expanse of sky, the most breathtaking mountain range, the bird with the most exotically beautiful plumage, the mysterious waters of the deep—James 1:18 tells us that we humans are His most prized possession.

When God conceived of Adam and Eve in the Garden of Eden, He already knew they would be different than the other living beings He'd designed. He created this man and woman in His own image (Genesis 1:27), beautifully complex and wondrously crafted. His relationship with the first humans was personal and intimate. God spent time with them in the Garden and had audible conversations with them. If only they hadn't

messed everything up by sinning, causing a separation between God and all of humanity.

But before creation, when God wrote His plan for us, He already knew the separation was coming. And He chose to send His true Word—His only Son, Jesus Christ, to make a way for Him to reclaim us and draw us into His presence for all eternity.

You are His prized possession, daughter of God! Claim that promise today and every day!

Creator God, when I'm feeling down on myself, keep reminding me what I mean to You. Amen.

THE HEART'S JUDGE

"The LORD doesn't see things the way you see them. People judge by outward appearance, but the LORD looks at the heart."
1 SAMUEL 16:7 NLT

Samuel had served God in many roles: judge, priest, prophet, counselor, and anointer of kings.

So when God sent Samuel to Bethlehem to find King Saul's replacement among Jesse's sons, Samuel thought he had a pretty good idea who was God's "type." He hadn't spent his entire life in service of the Lord without learning anything.

To Samuel, Jesse's firstborn son, Eliab—tall, strong, and handsome—seemed to be the obvious choice. But before Samuel could crack open the anointing oil, God warned him against judging on appearance alone.

God knows it's human nature—even for someone as devout as Samuel—to judge by how someone looks.

But appearance doesn't reveal the true self or a person's actual value. God judges on heart and character. And because only He can see what's on the inside, only He can judge fairly.

If you're like most women, your daily outer-beauty routine is almost second nature. But how about your *inner*-beauty routine? Are you putting in enough time to cultivate the true beauty God looks for?

God, examine my heart and give me a full report.
If there are ugly motives or hidden sins in the
recesses of my heart, help me clear them out.
Then fill me with Your pure and holy love. Amen.

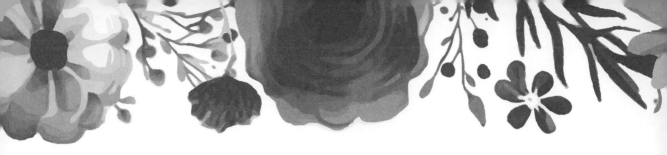

FAITH PLUS ACTION

Now someone may argue, "Some people have faith;
others have good deeds." But I say, "How can you
show me your faith if you don't have good deeds?
I will show you my faith by my good deeds."
James 2:18 NLT

Imagine your first appointment with a dentist. After introducing herself and motioning to her diploma on the wall, she pulls out a tray of dental implements and tells you what each one does. Then she shakes your hand, wishes you well, and tells you to pay the receptionist on the way out.

If she never actually *did* any work on your teeth, is she really a dentist?

If we never display good works in our lives, are we really Christians?

While scripture clearly tell us that our good deeds cannot earn salvation (Ephesians 2:8–9), James tells

us that true faith *always* results in a changed life and good deeds.

James uses Abraham to make his point: "Don't you remember that our ancestor Abraham was shown to be right with God by his actions when he offered his son Isaac on the altar? You see, his faith and his actions worked together. His actions made his faith complete" (James 2:21–22 NLT).

Is your faith resulting in actions? If you're not sure, find a trusted Christian friend who is busy doing God's work and jump in!

Jesus, I want an action-packed faith that You can use to do big things. I will not be idle. Amen.

A GENEROUS AND GRACIOUS LORD

Oh, how generous and gracious our Lord was! He filled me with the faith and love that come from Christ Jesus.
1 TIMOTHY 1:14 NLT

In his letter to Timothy, the apostle Paul reminds us of his storied past. Before his encounter with Jesus in Acts 9, Paul was raised to be a zealous Pharisee like his father (Acts 23:6). His Jewish heritage, discipline, and passion was unmatched (Philippians 3:4–6). He hated and actively persecuted Christians. He had active roles in their death and imprisonment (Acts 8:1).

Yet because of God's love and compassion, Paul was forgiven much, and he knew his story was a beautiful example of the saving grace of the Father—of the transforming power of God's love. If God saved this man with

such a wicked heart full of evil *and* God trusted Paul to be a messenger of Christ, then God can do the same for you too.

Today, let go of the guilt of your past. God is ready and willing to forgive and accept you. God forgave Paul and used Paul mightily for His kingdom. God can and will use you mightily too!

Father God, today I'm releasing the shame of my past. I'm lifting my eyes to You and asking for forgiveness and freedom from the guilt I've felt for so long. Raise me up and remind me that I'm Your cherished daughter who can and will be involved in mighty things in Your kingdom.

JESUS THE GREAT EMANCIPATOR

Jesus replied, "I tell you the truth, everyone who sins is a slave of sin. A slave is not a permanent member of the family, but a son is part of the family forever. So if the Son sets you free, you are truly free."

John 8:34–36 NLT

Jesus' Jewish followers were confused. *They* didn't need to be set free. It was their ancestors who had been slaves—not them. That was behind them now, so how would the truth set them free? Free from what?

One word, three letters: S-I-N.

Sin's grip on our minds, hearts, and bodies is stronger than any link of chain used by the cruelest slave master. It begins with a temptation that leads to a decision to act in a way that separates us from God and results in death. Try as we might, we cannot wish,

bargain, buy, or fight our way out of sin's slavery.

But just as Jesus' followers begin to understand their own sin-slave status, He gives them an important reminder: slaves aren't born into sin the way a son or daughter is born into a family. Slavery is not permanent if an emancipator comes. And Jesus is that Great Emancipator, the one who, because of His death on the cross, frees sin's most captive slave.

Jesus, unlock these chains of sin and set me free. I want to change my status from sin's slave to God's daughter. Amen.

EXTREME TRANSFORMATION: SPIRITUAL EDITION

*"Speak a prophetic message and say, 'This is what the Sovereign L*ORD *says: Come, O breath, from the four winds! Breathe into these dead bodies so they may live again.'"*

EZEKIEL 37:9 NLT

Everyone loves a transformation—especially an *extreme* transformation. Pounds lost amount to a triple-digit number; a modest, dumpy house morphs into an immaculate model home; long, wavy hair becomes a perky straight bob.

Ezekiel's vision in chapter 37 illustrates an extreme transformation that held a promise for God's people yesterday and for us today. The dry bones are a picture of the Jews in captivity—scattered and spiritually

dead. At the time of the vision, Ezekiel felt he *was* speaking to the dead as he preached to the exiles because they rarely responded to his message. But those bones responded! And just as God brought life to the long-dead bones, He would bring life again to His spiritually dead people.

If you've been a Christian for a while, you've probably experienced some seasons of being spiritually alive and others on spiritual life support. If God can take long-dead, dried-up, crusty bones and transform them into living, breathing people, have hope that He *can* and *will* bring your faith back from the dead. Ask Him to start that extreme transformation *now*!

God, I'm ready for a change. Breathe new life into me so I may live fully in You again! Amen.

ACCEPTING ADVICE

Pride leads to conflict; those who take advice are wise. . . . People who despise advice are asking for trouble; those who respect a command will succeed.
PROVERBS 13:10, 13 NLT

I was wrong. There are few phrases in the English language more difficult to say.

Why? Because admitting we don't know everything requires humility. It's acknowledging a personal failure. It's listening to advice when our pride is already stinging.

Pride is an ingredient in every conflict. It can stir up indignant feelings and lash out. Pride is a know-it-all just waiting for someone to dare suggest there might be a better way. Pride is impatient and often rude. Pride preserves self above anything else.

Humility, on the other hand, is a calming salve in arguments and can help heal a relationship. Displaying

a humble attitude takes work, but with it comes peace, and a reassurance that we *don't* have to know it all or be right all the time. Humility helps us see others as Jesus sees them.

Be open to the advice of people you respect and admire. Ask for help when you need it, and be receptive to tough love, even if you don't ask for it. When we open ourselves up to wise advice from others, we're open to God's instructions. True wisdom is hearing God's guidance through His Word and following it.

*Create in me a humble heart, O God. I welcome
the loving instruction in Your Word and am
open to hearing Your wisdom from others.*

THE HARD WHYS

As Jesus was walking along, he saw a man who had been blind from birth. "Rabbi," his disciples asked him, "why was this man born blind? Was it because of his own sins or his parents' sins?" "It was not because of his sins or his parents' sins," Jesus answered. "This happened so the power of God could be seen in him."

JOHN 9:1–3 NLT

Why was a baby born blind only to grow up to beg along the side of the road? Jesus' disciples wondered. A punishment for his sin?

Jesus' response must've surprised them. This man had been born blind so that God's power would be displayed in his healing. After Jesus healed his blindness, the now-seeing man repeatedly told the story of a Jewish rabbi named Jesus who'd restored his sight with mud, saliva, and a wash in the Pool of Siloam. His testimony allowed more people—including his neighbors

and a group of Pharisees investigating Jesus—to hear about and see God's power firsthand.

What hard whys are in your life right now? Maybe the *why* is less important than the *how*. How is God displaying His power to you and to others around you? And how is your testimony of Him being a kind, merciful, and powerful God pointing others to Him?

Healer God, today I'm trusting that You are working everything in my life—the easy and the difficult—for Your glory. Show me how to testify of Your power, God. Amen.

IT'S CLEAR

"Why, that's very strange!" the man replied. "He healed my eyes, and yet you don't know where he comes from? We know that God doesn't listen to sinners, but he is ready to hear those who worship him and do his will. Ever since the world began, no one has been able to open the eyes of someone born blind. If this man were not from God, he couldn't have done it."

JOHN 9:30–33 NLT

The man Jesus healed from blindness already knew the Rabbi who put mud and saliva on his face was no ordinary rabbi. When the Pharisees summoned the healed man to answer questions, looking to find evidence in Jesus' wrongdoing, he couldn't believe his ears.

Were these religious leaders so blind they couldn't see that Jesus was doing God's work? What was clear to him was obscured by the Pharisees' hard hearts.

When you've experienced the life-changing power

of God, you see His presence and power in daily life. Prayer, scripture reading, and listening to God only adds to your awareness of Him.

Who do you know who could be encouraged by your story of God's work in your life? Remember that although it's not your job to change hard hearts—only the Holy Spirit can do that—your personal, relatable stories can go a long way in beginning to soften a heart.

Father, use me to encourage someone
going through a difficult time. Amen.

ELIAB'S JEALOUSY

When David's oldest brother, Eliab, heard David talking to the men, he was angry. "What are you doing around here anyway?" he demanded. "What about those few sheep you're supposed to be taking care of? I know about your pride and deceit. You just want to see the battle!"

1 SAMUEL 17:28 NLT

Eliab didn't like David's youthful zeal for going to battle for the Lord. The older brother viewed David as just a child, one who needed to go home to do his little job of tending the needs of his flock.

Newbie, on-fire Christians can be so annoying with their excitement and passion. They need to take a breath and settle down.

Ever felt this way, longtime woman of faith?

Instead of squelching the fire in a new Christian's heart, what if you used her enthusiasm to propel you

on to deeper faith and greater work for God's kingdom? If Eliab had been successful in sending David home, the shepherd boy and soon-to-be king would not have defeated Goliath, leaving the Israelites to continue suffering at the hands of the Philistines.

What sparks do you see around you that you can fan into flames? What will you do to keep the cares of the world from dampening or putting them out?

God, add fuel to my fire and restore my passion for You and for Your work. Give me a pure heart that willingly comes alongside others who are ignited with love and excitement for You. Amen.

HARD QUESTIONS

"Teacher," they said to Jesus, "this woman was caught in the act of adultery. The law of Moses says to stone her. What do you say?"
<small>JOHN 8:4 NLT</small>

The teachers of the law and the Pharisees didn't care one bit about the woman they'd dragged before Jesus. She was simply a way to test and trap Him (John 8:6). They held up the Old Testament law that says adultery warrants death by stoning, daring Jesus to disagree. With white knuckles firmly grasping rocks, what they *really* wanted to do was hurl the stones at Jesus, the man some people were beginning to murmur was the Messiah.

But Jesus wasn't tricked by their trap. He didn't seem riled by the question or unsettled by the mob, and He didn't retaliate by calling out their hypocrisy or naming specific sins and vices of each one. Instead,

He turned the focus from their legalism of keeping the ancient law to His law of compassionate love by reminding them no one has the right to judge another's guilt.

As a Christian, there may be times when you're assaulted by questions from hard hearts who are hoping to make your faith in God look foolish. Don't fall into the trap of angry retaliation. Instead, take a breath and choose the path of the compassionate love of Jesus.

Jesus, when I feel my faith being attacked, give me the strength to pause and react in love. Amen.

ONE AND DONE

And just as each person is destined to die once and after that comes judgment, so also Christ was offered once for all time as a sacrifice to take away the sins of many people.
HEBREWS 9:27–28 NLT

Before Adam and Eve disobeyed God's instruction, His creation was whole and perfect—poised to spend eternity in the presence of the Creator. But when sin entered the world in the Garden of Eden, death entered too. That mortal wound to the relationship between God and humans resulted in spiritual death that we tried to fix with the priest and sacrifice system in the Old Testament. But even a lifetime of blood sacrifice and ritual wasn't good enough to heal that relationship. Only Jesus dying on the cross could provide complete restoration.

Each of us will die physically, but Christ died on the

cross, once for all (Hebrews 9:26), so we would not have to die spiritually. If we have accepted His gift of grace, He has forgiven our past sin; He has given us the Holy Spirit to help us deal with present sin; He stands for us in heaven as our High Priest (9:24); and He promises to return (9:28) and raise us to eternal life in God's presence where sin will be no more.

Jesus, I am eagerly awaiting Your salvation. Thank You for making the perfect way for me to live with You in the Father's presence forever. Amen.

THE HIDDEN PATH

Your road led through the sea,
your pathway through the mighty waters—
a pathway no one knew was there!
PSALM 77:19 NLT

For some people, it's unnerving to not see the path ahead. Airplane travel is a real challenge for passengers who can't deal with not seeing out the front of the cabin. They're the ones who prefer to drive or call forever dibs on shotgun. They need to see where they're going.

The Israelites found themselves unable to see an escape on the shore of the Red Sea. With Pharaoh's army hot on their heels, not only couldn't they see a way ahead, but there *literally* was no road ahead. But God's pathway was there, and He revealed it in a mighty miracle by parting the waters and giving His people a bone-dry avenue of escape.

So when you find yourself on the shore with seemingly no path to take or at a crossroads with multiple ways ahead, stop and look at your surroundings. Ask God to guide you. Take the time to dig your way into scripture. Seek godly advice from mature Christians. Then rest assured the Lord will set you on His perfect pathway, even (or especially) if that means parting waters or moving mountains.

Way-Maker God, thank You for bringing me this far. I need Your help to find the next step in the journey. Make Your way evident and obvious so I am confident in my steps. Amen.

(DON'T) FAKE IT
TILL YOU MAKE IT

The wicked bluff their way through,
but the virtuous think before they act.
PROVERBS 21:29 NLT

Do you know anyone who is really good at baloney? Not completely dissimilar to actual bologna, the lunch box sandwich meat made up of leftover scraps, verbal baloney is the made-up kind of nonsense that consists of half-truths and bluffs, often used to get the upper hand in a situation or to make the speaker seem smarter than someone else.

Proverbs 21:29 tells us it's the wicked who baloney their way through life, unprepared for the challenges that inevitably come. But the virtuous *think* before they *act*.

So on a practical level, how can we be more

virtuous and less baloneyous? First, follow the wisdom of Proverbs. Take a breath. Think. Be transparent and admit when you *don't* have an answer or know what to do, and be willing to think and pray on it. Another way to stay on the virtuous track is to imprint God's Word on your heart and mind. Then if you're caught unprepared in a challenging situation or conversation, His truth is more likely to be on the tip of the tongue, ready to be offered in love.

Jesus, I know I'm the kind of person who wants to always have an answer, who always knows what to do. But I also admit that isn't always the case. Give me patience to act and react virtuously in a way that honors You always.

LONG FUSE

You, O God, are both tender and kind, not easily angered, immense in love, and you never, never quit.
PSALM 86:15 MSG

We all know someone who has a short fuse. The one who, at the smallest traffic delay or offense, loses her temper. Or turns red if she has to wait at the store checkout or gets a glare from a fellow shopper. She's the one others have to watch their words around for fear of setting her off.

Thankfully, the Bible says God has a long fuse—that He's slow to get angry (Exodus 34:6; Numbers 14:18; Nehemiah 9:17; Psalm 103:8; Joel 2:13; Jonah 4:2; Nahum 1:3). Yet does the fact that God has lots of patience mean we should give ourselves a pass when it comes to sin? Certainly not!

God's desire is for our salvation through Jesus Christ and adopting as many children into His family who'll

accept His gift of grace. He knows we aren't perfect—but His love is.

Ask God to show you where you might need to repent, remembering He's not angry. He's just waiting in compassion and mercy to give you the full life He's designed for you.

God, You've every right to get frustrated with me when I mess up, but Your patient mercy and love is greater than Your anger. Clean my hands and face and purify my heart, Father. I don't want any sin to stand between us. Amen.

SERVANT LEADERS

"Those who are the greatest among you should take the lowest rank, and the leader should be like a servant."

LUKE 22:26 NLT

When Jesus' disciples started arguing about who among them was the greatest, the Messiah must've sighed and shook His head. It's one thing for His sermons to go in one ear and out the other, but He'd been practicing what He was preaching, and they *still* didn't get it! His teaching truly was radically upside down to them. Nowhere else on earth did the disciples see powerful leaders who were humble servants.

By being a servant—choosing to honor others above Himself—Jesus demonstrated just one aspect of the upside-down nature of God's kingdom. The first will be last and the last will be first (Matthew 19:30). To have new life in Christ, one must give up one's life

(Matthew 16:24–25). Return hate with love (Romans 12:19–21). True wealth results from giving generously (Luke 6:38).

Not one aspect of Jesus' teaching is easy; each rubs against the grain of our selfish desires. But they are surprisingly simple. And the rewards of doing as Jesus said (and as He does) are immeasurable—both as a peaceful present and as a joyful future.

Jesus, fix my vision to see and fully understand Your right-side up kingdom. When my sinful heart wants to flip upside-down with the world, renew me and strengthen me. I will serve. I will love. I will give. Amen.

THE COURAGE TO SPEAK UP (OR NOT)

There was a lot of grumbling about him among the crowds. Some argued, "He's a good man," but others said, "He's nothing but a fraud who deceives the people." But no one had the courage to speak favorably about him in public, for they were afraid of getting in trouble with the Jewish leaders.

JOHN 7:12–13 NLT

Judea was abuzz with rumors that Jesus was there in secret, trying to stay out of public view (John 7:10).

Some people said quietly among themselves, "He's a good man, and we need more like Him."

Others proclaimed more loudly so the Jewish leaders could hear, "He's a fraud and a liar and he's pulling the wool over all our eyes!"

Have you ever known what's right but were too afraid

to speak up? Whether it's fear of public ridicule or the possibility of losing a position, a friendship, or something else, there are lots of reasons to remain silent. Speaking up takes courage. But it also takes wisdom to know when and when not to speak. So before setting up your soapbox:

1. Pray and ask God what He wants you to do.

2. Seek counsel in scripture and from godly friends/ family.

3. In all things, love.

*Father, when I need to stand up for what's right,
give me the courage and the words to use.
And when I need to remain silent, give
me peace as I keep my mouth shut.*

IF ONLY

When Mary arrived and saw Jesus, she fell at his feet and said, "Lord, if only you had been here, my brother would not have died."

JOHN 11:32 NLT

Nobody wants to live with regrets, but we all suffer from a case of the "could haves," "should haves," and "would haves" every now and then. Decisions and plans would be a lot easier to make if we could know what's going to happen.

In John 11, Jesus finds Mary overflowing with regret when He arrives after her brother, Lazarus, died. "Lord, if only you had been here, my brother would not have died," she sobbed at Jesus' feet.

But Jesus knew something Mary hadn't yet realized: there are no "if onlys" in God's kingdom. No regrets. No "should haves," "could haves," or "would haves." What the suffering Mary and her sister, Martha, were going

through was temporary. And in a matter of minutes, the Son of God would be glorified, bringing eternal joy to a mourning family once He raised Lazarus from the dead.

Do you have any regrets you're currently struggling through? Lay those "if onlys" at the feet of Jesus. He knows what's next, and He can take any situation (even death!) and use it for His glory—and your joy.

Regrets, Jesus, I have a few. Forgive me and help me forgive myself. Please use these missteps to Your glory—to further Your kingdom here and for eternity. Amen.

EXTRAVAGANT GRATITUDE

*Then Mary took about a pint of pure nard,
an expensive perfume; she poured it on Jesus'
feet and wiped his feet with her hair.*

JOHN 12:3 NIV

As Christians, we spend a lot of time counting the cost of Jesus' sacrifice on the cross. It's the cornerstone of our faith, so we rightly should remember His death and resurrection. But while it's true that there's nothing we can do to repay Jesus, that doesn't mean we can't show extravagant gratitude for all He has done—even to the point of our seeming ridiculous to others.

For Mary, extravagant gratitude meant spending what perhaps was her life's savings to purchase a jar of the most expensive perfume she could find. Imagine Mary's excitement to present Jesus with such a loving

gift. With each ounce she poured upon His feet and wiped with her hair, she celebrated the love He had already poured out on her family, through His teaching, encouraging, challenging, and most of all saving her brother, Lazarus, from the grave. Such extravagant love from the Rabbi deserved the most extravagant gratitude she could muster.

What does extravagant gratitude look like in your life? Don't let naysayers keep you from displaying your thankfulness (see John 12:4–5). Jesus Christ is worthy and deserving of all your praise!

Jesus, I know there is nothing I can do to repay You. Please accept my offering of extravagant gratitude, and may it be a blessing to You. Amen.

UP TO THIS POINT

Samuel then took a large stone and placed it between the towns of Mizpah and Jeshanah. He named it Ebenezer (which means "the stone of help"), for he said, "Up to this point the LORD has helped us!"
1 SAMUEL 7:12 NLT

Some seasons of life are just plain hard. In these tough times, it's easy to let doubts seep in and faith to waver. *Why is God letting this happen? Does He even care? Where is He?*

In trying times, follow the prophet Samuel's example and set up an Ebenezer. An Ebenezer can be anything that reminds you that up until now, God has helped you, and He will be faithful in continuing to help! Maybe that means writing an entry in your calendar app or a journal, recording the date when you felt God's presence or saw His provision in a difficult situation. Maybe it's planting a tree or placing a rock in a garden.

Maybe it's crafting a bracelet or necklace charm with a date etched on it—a possible conversation starter to talk to others about when God has helped you.

God's help is ever-present. And you become more aware of that help when you're looking for it. Today, remember and thank God for the things He has done, is doing, and will do.

God, I'm not worthy of Your help, yet You offer it freely and generously. I praise You for each milestone of Your provision in my life. Amen.

ETERNAL BENEFITS

"Physical training is good, but training for godliness is much better, promising benefits in this life and in the life to come."
1 TIMOTHY 4:8 NLT

What do conditioning for a marathon, rehearsing for a performance, and purposefully becoming more like Christ all have in common? Each takes a journey, a process, discipline, a plan, and a commitment to keep making progress toward a goal.

All of these things are good, but only one has eternal benefits: training for godliness.

Spiritual training, like physical training, doesn't happen by accident. We won't spontaneously become more like Jesus in our thoughts and actions. But we do know some ways that will help us get there. First, let go of things that get in the way of that training. Consider what parts of your schedule you could cut out to make

time to spend with God. Use 1 Corinthians 10:23 as a litmus test: "You say, 'I am allowed to do anything'—but not everything is good for you. You say, 'I am allowed to do anything'—but not everything is beneficial" (NLT).

Second, choose one step to take in your spiritual walk, and then do it. Start small. Commit to opening up God's Word every day or spend a minute or two in prayer. Flex those muscles, learn the motions, and then gradually add more.

Father, be my coach in my spiritual training.
I need Your encouragement and strength
as I journey through this life of faith.

A LOVING FATHER'S CORRECTION

Those who spare the rod of discipline hate their children. Those who love their children care enough to discipline them.

PROVERBS 13:24 NLT

No loving mom/aunt/grandma takes joy in disciplining a child. Yet when we correct the children in our lives, we show them that we love them. Even when a kid bucks and tantrums her way through discipline, a loving adult continues, knowing that discipline helps move her in a direction that will benefit her now and as she grows and matures.

Consider the words of Proverbs 13:24 where God is the parent and you are His child. How do you respond to God's correction? Do you scream and stomp? Whine and wail? Or can you step back and learn to see it as

a deeply loving gesture of a good Father who corrects and disciplines those He loves (Revelation 3:19)? Paul puts discipline in greater context in Hebrews 12:11: "No discipline is enjoyable while it is happening—it's painful! But afterward there will be a peaceful harvest of right living for those who are trained in this way" (NLT).

God takes no joy in disciplining His children. Pray and ask God to soften your heart toward His correction. Whether it comes today, tomorrow, or sometime in the future, know that it will result in blessings on your life!

Father, although a hard prayer to pray,
I'll welcome Your discipline when I need
Your loving correction. Even when it doesn't
feel nice, I'll still know You love me.

HANDPICKED

God the Father knew you and chose you long ago, and his Spirit has made you holy. As a result, you have obeyed him and have been cleansed by the blood of Jesus Christ.

1 Peter 1:2 nlt

No matter how beautiful, accomplished, athletic, smart, capable, creative, or loving we might be, we've all experienced rejection: didn't get the job; didn't make the team; didn't receive the scholarship; didn't get asked to the dance; didn't get the leadership appointment; didn't get a second date; got cheated on; never received an invitation; didn't make first chair. . . .

Try as we might to pretend we don't care when we're not chosen, rejection hurts. A lot. Young or old, green or experienced, simple or sophisticated, rejection makes us question our worth and wonder why we even try.

Before Jesus came, only the nation of Israel could claim to be God's chosen people. But because of Christ, all believers—Jews and Gentiles—belong to God. Here's a beautiful truth in scripture, sister: When you were born, God had already chosen and accepted you. Your salvation and security rest in the free and merciful choice of your almighty God, and nothing can take away His love for those who believe in Him (Romans 8:38–39).

Father, You chose me first, but I choose You now and forever. Thank You for wanting me even if others reject me. You hold my heart, God. I trust You with it. Amen.

CONTENTMENT

True godliness with contentment is itself great wealth. After all, we brought nothing with us when we came into the world, and we can't take anything with us when we leave it.

1 TIMOTHY 6:6–7 NLT

As children, we learn the difference between *needs* and *wants.* We need food and clothes and shelter and love. Wants? Well, wants can be anything and often *everything.* Our wants can balloon into an Amazon wishlist a mile long, just waiting for the day we swipe BUY NOW. Because those things will make us feel better, right?

After the initial jolt of dopamine that comes with the thrill of a purchase, we realize *things* don't bring peace or lasting happiness. What brings real peace and joy is contentment. The importance of this spiritual discipline can't be overlooked. For contentment coupled with godliness equals "great wealth." Why? Because

when we live in a state of gratitude, trusting God will supply all we need, we realize just how immensely blessed we are. Paul writes, "Teach those who are rich in this world not to be proud and not to trust in their money, which is so unreliable. Their trust should be in God, who richly gives us all we need for our enjoyment" (1 Timothy 6:17 NLT).

Do you feel anxious, always striving for the next thing, for more? Pause. Rest, relying on God's unending strength and love.

Father, calm my heart and help me to live every day grateful for Your surpassing goodness to me.

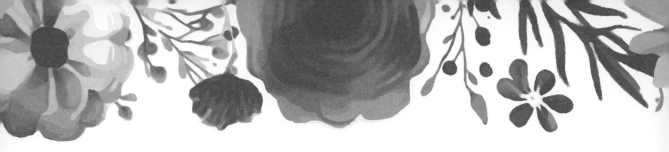

REBORN INTO GOD'S FAMILY

To all who did receive him, who believed in his name, he gave the right to become children of God, who were born, not of blood nor of the will of the flesh nor of the will of man, but of God.

JOHN 1:12–13 ESV

The nine months leading up to the birth of a baby are filled with excitement, expectation, anticipation, and a whole lot of joy in a family. From nursery prep to acquiring baby gear, planning a shower, and stocking up on diapers and wipes, there's hope and promise in every moment. *Who will this tiny person be? What will she become? Who will he take after? Where will her strengths and passions lie?*

As much as your family may have looked forward to your physical birth, God's anticipation for your rebirth

into His family is even greater. His call to you began when He first thought of you. He claimed you for *His* family and marked you for rebirth. He loved as you came into the world an infant and grew first physically, then spiritually as you began to understand His love and loved Him in return.

Then came that glorious day when you took the step of faith and publicly declared that Jesus is the Son of God and Lord of your life. You became a Father/daughter duo for eternity. Can you hear the applause of heaven (Luke 15:10)?

You are my good Father. I am Your grateful child. I love You! Amen.

OUR ADVOCATE
AND RESCUER

*"May the L*ORD* therefore judge which of us is right and punish the guilty one. He is my advocate, and he will rescue me from your power!"*

1 SAMUEL 24:15 NLT

David had every right to take revenge on King Saul. For Saul had publicly declared his plans to kill David *and* had enlisted the help of three thousand of his elite troops to hunt David down in the wilderness. So when Saul happened to take a pit stop in the very cave where David was hiding, David knew it was his best chance to strike.

But he didn't. All he did was cut a piece from Saul's robe. And even that made him feel guilty (1 Samuel 24:5).

We might be tempted to think David a better man

than Saul, but the truth is that both kings were sinful, fallen humans who each messed up big-time, in his own way. The difference was that David had a personal relationship with the Lord—a God he trusted to rescue him in times of distress.

What wrongs have been done to you that you need to let go of? What hope of revenge do you hold in your heart? Ask Jesus to remove it; then replace it with the peace of knowing He will champion you.

Advocate God, when I am feeling the icy fingers of revenge creep into my heart, stand for me. Rescue me and put my feet on solid ground. Amen.

GET ME OFF THIS SLIP 'N' SLIDE

Don't slip back into your old ways of living to satisfy your own desires. You didn't know any better then. But now you must be holy in everything you do, just as God who chose you is holy.

1 Peter 1:14–15 NLT

Black ice is invisible. You don't even realize it's there until you're on your back, staring up at the sky, wondering what happened. Old temptations and pitfalls from your old life can make you lose your footing in the same way, tripping you up, pulling you back to your old ways of thinking and acting. The Christianese term for that is *backsliding*.

But once we're made new in Christ, we're to be holy like our heavenly Father. Holiness means being totally devoted to God, set aside for His special use and set

apart from sin and its influence. Our priorities must be the same as His.

Sounds hard, right?

The truth is, you can't become holy on your own power. Don't use the excuse that you can't help slip-sliding back into sin. God gives you His Holy Spirit to help you overcome temptation. So call on God's power and Spirit to put you on stable footing. He is faithful and will deliver you every day!

Father, I don't want to return to my old ways.
Give me the power to resist my evil desire.
Bring friends into my life who'll reach out
a hand to keep me from sliding. Amen.

HERITAGE OF FAITH

I remember your genuine faith, for you share the faith that first filled your grandmother Lois and your mother, Eunice. And I know that same faith continues strong in you.
2 Timothy 1:5–7 nlt

If you've ever done any ancestry research, you may have uncovered connections to your family heritage that you didn't expect. Family trees often contain certain traits, careers, passions, or skills that play a big role in family histories, binding families together across generations.

In a similar way, our faith-family tree connects us in our common bond with other believers in a heritage that spans to the beginning of creation. It doesn't matter whether your biological ancestors passed down a faith to you; if you have accepted Jesus as your Savior, you are a part of the family tree of God. You are part of

the body of Christ. You are the adopted sister of Jesus Christ and daughter of the King of kings and Lord of lords. The eternal spirit of power, love, and stability lives in you. Because of that you cannot be picked, plucked, cut out, or uprooted from this eternal tree.

If you have children, help them grow in and graft onto the tree of faith, just like Timothy's mother and grandmother did. Although it's made up of imperfect individuals, the family of God is eternal and made perfect in Him.

God, I am thankful to be a part of Your family tree of faith that spans across all borders and generations.

TURN US, GOD

*Turn us again to yourself, O God of Heaven's
Armies. Make your face shine down upon
us. Only then will we be saved.*

PSALM 80:7 NLT

Compared with many other species, we humans have mediocre peripheral vision—what we can see that's outside the center of our gaze. The closer something is to the center of our gaze, the sharper and more clearly we can see it. The farther to the left and right, our vision becomes blurrier. (A typical visual field is about 170 degrees around—slightly less than halfway around your head.)*

The psalmist understood the importance of keeping God at the center of one's gaze. So he asked the Lord to turn the focus of the Israelites back to Him and away from the distractions of other gods and idols. For it's not enough to have a slightly blurry God in the

periphery. He must be in the sharpest vision plane; and other good, but nonessential, parts of life must be in the periphery.

As you think about these things, remember that God doesn't move; it's you who turn away. Today, ask God to turn you back to Him. And as He comes into focus, note His eyes full of love for you.

Father, once again I've been distracted by the temptations of this world and You've become blurry. Forgive me and turn me back to You. I long to see Your face shine down on me. Amen.

*www.eyehealthweb.com/peripheral-vision/

KNOW YOUR PURPOSE

"You will become pregnant and give birth to a son, and his hair must never be cut. For he will be dedicated to God as a Nazirite from birth. He will begin to rescue Israel from the Philistines."

JUDGES 13:5 NLT

Baby Samson came with an instruction manual *and* a prophecy:

1. Don't cut his hair.

2. Dedicate him to God as a Nazirite.

3. Someday he will begin to rescue Israel from the Philistines.

This infant grew to be an amazingly strong man with superhero-like qualities who, despite his own shortcomings and sin (read Judges 13–16 for his full story), ultimately fulfilled his prebirth prophecy.

Do you ever wish that an angel had not only given

your parents an instruction manual but proclaimed your purpose before your birth? If you've ever struggled with meaning—what you're meant to do on earth—you're not alone.

Although you may sometimes feel small and insignificant and unable to do anything really worthwhile in this messed-up world, know this: when God designed your life, He didn't roll the dice and arbitrarily place you. No, He crafted your unique position—the years you live, the family you belong to, the career you pursue, the friends you choose, your passions and abilities—to give you the opportunity to make an everlasting impact on the world. Big, earth-changing revivals or small, personal kindnesses alike—you can make a difference.

God, please show me how to make an everlasting impact today. Use me, Father. Amen.

LIVING STONES

You are coming to Christ, who is the living cornerstone of God's temple. He was rejected by people, but he was chosen by God for great honor. And you are living stones that God is building into his spiritual temple.

1 PETER 2:4–5 NLT

Stonemasonry is more than simply stacking rocks. To become a master stonemason takes years of training to build beautiful, structurally sound walls that stand the test of time. A mason carefully chooses each stone for its shape, size, and composition, and he fits them as meticulously as pieces in a jigsaw puzzle.

Peter describes the church as a living, spiritual house, with Christ as the foundation, Cornerstone, and each believer as a stone. This picture, just like Paul's description of the church as a body in Ephesians 4:15–16, emphasizes the importance of community.

Just as one stone does not make a temple, one bone does not make a body. Peter and Paul agree: we need one another.

In our individualistic society, it is easy to forget our interdependence with other Christians. But when God calls us to a task, He is also calling others to work with us. If we work together, God can exponentially multiply our efforts.

So look for those people who are passionately pursuing God. Then join them.

Jesus, thank You for surrounding me with Your beautiful, living stones. Bring us together in unity to be set apart as God's holy temple. Amen.

ASKING FOR WHAT GOD WANTS

But the people wouldn't listen to Samuel. "No!"
they said. "We will have a king to rule us! Then
we'll be just like all the other nations. Our king
will rule us and lead us and fight our battles."
1 SAMUEL 8:19–20 MSG

Have you ever tried reasoning with a two-year-old? Listing eight compelling reasons why the toddler shouldn't dump a shoebox of LEGO blocks into the toilet will get you nowhere.

The Jews were as irrational as two-year-olds when they wanted a king. Samuel gave them a laundry list of the consequences of having a king (1 Samuel 8:10–18), yet their demand grew louder.

God is a generous Father who will give good gifts when asked (Matthew 7:11), but He is also a Father who

knows what will benefit you and what will harm you. A toddler may want a box of matches with all his heart, but no loving father will hand them to her.

So how do you work in harmony with God's generosity? By living in His will and asking for good gifts that are in line with His kingdom: gifts to love others, share the good news, feed the hungry, care for the sick. Ask for the opportunity, tools, and the means to carry out these things, and God's generosity will overflow.

Generous Father, show me Your will so
I know I am offering up requests that
bring You joy to answer. Amen.

TRUE FREEDOM

For you have been called to live in freedom,
my brothers and sisters. But don't use your
freedom to satisfy your sinful nature. Instead,
use your freedom to serve one another in love.

GALATIANS 5:13 NLT

"I do what I want."

This tongue-in-cheek definition of freedom may sound like something from the mouth of a three-year-old, but it's essentially what the world says it means to be free.

The problem is that we will often use that freedom to satisfy our own desires. We will do whatever feels good to benefit ourselves. To indulge until we are sick. To manipulate people and situations to make them better for us. To make ourselves better off at any cost.

Instead, the apostle Paul encourages us to elevate our thoughts and actions about freedom, writing in 1

Corinthians 10:23–24: "You say, 'I am allowed to do anything'—but not everything is beneficial. Don't be concerned for your own good but for the good of others" (NLT).

When we use our freedom to love others, we're not only following God's second greatest command (Mark 12:31), we are also experiencing His love for us more powerfully. Freedom that serves in love cannot be revoked. True freedom isn't found in earthly governments or constitutions; it's only found in the unending power of Christ's love for us that He demonstrated on the cross.

I will not take my freedom for granted, Jesus.
Make me worthy of such a privilege. Amen.

TWO SMALL COINS

"I tell you the truth," Jesus said, "this poor widow has given more than all the rest of them. For they have given a tiny part of their surplus, but she, poor as she is, has given everything she has."

LUKE 21:3–4 NLT

Financial giving seems like a pretty simple transaction. Some person or organization has a need, and others give to fill that need. It's opening up a wallet and removing bills. It's swiping a card or tapping an app. On rare occasions, it's trying to remember the proper way to write a check. Not much different than any other time currency changes hands, right?

Wrong. Jesus doesn't just want our cold, hard cash. He wants our hearts to be involved in the giving. A generous spirit that honors God, Jesus says, gives sacrificially. It's about stretching ourselves to give out of gratefulness for what God has provided, whether we

have much or little.

When it comes down to it, God owns it all anyway. We are merely the caretakers of His resources. So the next time an opportunity to give arises, ask the supplier what He wants you to do. He can and will use you in a mighty way!

Generous supplier of my needs, forgive me when I act like my money is solely mine to hoard and squander. I want the resources You've blessed me with to be used to further Your kingdom. Show me how and where. Amen.

BEAUTIFUL MESSAGES

How beautiful on the mountains are the feet
of the messenger who brings good news,
the good news of peace and salvation,
the news that the God of Israel reigns!
Isaiah 52:7 nlt

The beauty of God's creation is all around. From the explosion of jewel-toned autumn leaves to the bubbling, infectious giggle of a preschooler, we can see God's joy, peace, and harmony—if we take the time to notice it.

Appreciating God's gifts is good. It anchors us deep in His unending love and reassures us of His presence, protection, and provision. But once we've grasped hold of this truth, it's time to share it with the people around us and fully experience the good news of peace and grace. You are an influencer. Each of us—CEOs of corporations to stay-at-home moms alike—have

an impact on our world. Our words and actions affect friends, coworkers, neighbors, and even perfect strangers we encounter each day.

You, lovely sister in Christ, have a beautiful message to share. Tell a friend what God's doing in your life. Talk about God's faithfulness in a difficult situation, how walking with Him made you unshakable. Encourage someone—just because. Ask God to saturate your soul with His love so that it overflows into your thoughts, conversations, and deeds.

Father, thank You for the opportunity to be Your messenger. Help me to live authentically, with a pure heart for Your ways. Give me eyes to see others the way You see them—as Your cherished children.

DISAPPEARING ACT

"Heaven and earth will disappear,
but my words will never disappear."
Luke 21:33 nlt

Even the smartest Bible scholars don't know the exact circumstances of Jesus' second coming. The when and the how will remain a mystery until it happens, but the *why* is no secret: God will redeem His creation.

Part of that redemption means the present heaven and earth will be replaced with a new heaven and a new earth, which the apostle John wrote about in Revelation 21. Jesus mentioned a similar disappearing act to His followers in Luke 21, probably causing some angst in the crowd. Yes, the evaporation of heaven and earth *seems* troubling, but Jesus followed that preface by saying *His words will never disappear*. That means God's holy Word and all the promises within it are

more real and eternal today than the ground beneath your feet.

When friends walk out, when a job goes up in smoke, when a loved one dies, when it feels as though heaven and earth are disappearing now, God's power, compassion, grace, love, authority, and dominion over all speak through His Word. Dig in, and hold on to the true source of hope.

Never-ending God, I read in Isaiah that "the grass withers and the flowers fall, but the word of our God endures forever" (40:8 NIV). Create in me a hunger to devour Your Word, and give me a fertile heart to receive it to grow good things.

EXPECT A MIRACLE

When Jesus looked up and saw a great crowd coming toward him, he said to Philip, "Where shall we buy bread for these people to eat?" He asked this only to test him, for he already had in mind what he was going to do. Philip answered him, "It would take more than half a year's wages to buy enough bread for each one to have a bite!"

John 6:5–7 niv

When Jesus asked Philip how they could feed the thousands of people coming to hear Him speak, Philip was at a loss. Jesus had no money, and neither did His disciples. But Jesus knew the miracle that was coming, and it had the power to change Philip's faith forever.

There are times in every Christian's life when Jesus presents him or her with a challenge—something that seems impossible—but it's really an opportunity for God's power to shine, making the impossible, possible.

What question do you hear Jesus asking? "How can we keep the homeless warm this winter?" Or, "How can we show love to children in the foster care system?"

If Jesus has put a need on your heart, He already has a way to move forward. If you're willing to be used for good and it's in God's will, He'll make it happen—on an enough-food-to-feed-more-than-five-thousand-people-with-just-five-loaves-and-two-fish scale!

Jesus, I expect a miracle.
Use me to bring it about. Amen.

OUR GREATER PURPOSE

"For I have come down from heaven, not to do my own will but the will of him who sent me."
JOHN 6:38 ESV

One trait of an exceptional boss is that she clearly communicates expectations and instructions to her employees. When a leader sets a goal and launches the trajectory toward that goal, it provides purpose and focus that point each person toward the same result, pushing one another toward the finish line.

Our heavenly Father is an exceptional, supernatural boss. He's all about building His kingdom. To that end He sent His Son to earth with a singular focus: to make a way to bring His children into grace.

Jesus understood God's plan in a personal way that gave Him a mission unlike any other human in the past

or in the future. Doing God's will meant that Jesus' actions and decisions had a greater purpose than His own human desires and temptations. For us, that means that we don't have to make an educated guess about what God's will is. God's written instruction for our lives comes down to four simple letters: L-O-V-E.

Take comfort in the fact that you're working for All of Creation's Greatest Boss. Follow His instruction, carry out His will, and live a life of greater purpose.

God, thank You for the gift of Your Word. Forgive me for taking it for granted. Give me a Christlike desire to lay aside my own will and do only Yours. Amen.

SCRIPTURE INDEX

OLD TESTAMENT

LOOKING FOR MORE ENCOURAGEMENT?

Worry Less, Pray More Large Print

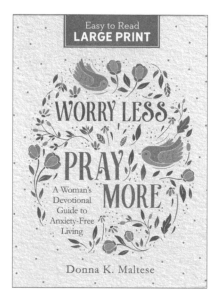

This purposeful devotional guide features 180 readings and prayers designed to help alleviate your worries as you learn to live in the peace of the Almighty God, who offers calm for your anxiety-filled soul. Inspired by Philippians 4:6–7, *Worry Less, Pray More* reinforces the truth that with God, you can live anxiety-free every single day—whether you worry about your work, relationships, bills, the turmoil of the world, or something else.

Paperback / 978-1-63609-422-9